LEADERS' DECISION MAKING AND NEUROSCIENCE

LEADERS' DECISION MAKING AND NEUROSCIENCE

What Are You thinking?

BY

YINYING WANG
Georgia State University, USA

United Kingdom – North America – Japan – India
Malaysia – China

Emerald Publishing Limited
Emerald Publishing, Floor 5, Northspring, 21-23 Wellington Street, Leeds LS1 4DL

First edition 2024

Reprints and permissions service
Contact: www.copyright.com

British Library Cataloguing in Publication Data
A catalogue record for this book is available from the British Library

ISBN: 978-1-83797-387-3 (Print)
ISBN: 978-1-83797-386-6 (Online)
ISBN: 978-1-83797-388-0 (Epub)

INVESTOR IN PEOPLE

CONTENTS

1

INTRODUCTION: LEADERS' BRAIN AS A DECISION-MAKING ORGAN

What exactly is leadership? At its core, leadership is about motivating a group of people to achieve shared goals. To understand leadership, we need to answer a fundamental question: Why do people behave the way they do? Traditionally, leadership has been studied through a behavioral lens – an examination of leaders' behaviors. Yet, this behavioral approach invites a further query: Where does behavior come from? Behavior, both leaders' behavior and how people respond to it, is an outward manifestation of a decision made in the human brain. Think of leadership as a tree, where visible branches and stems represent observable behaviors. Still, there is a substantial part that remains invisible – the root system, which is like intricate mental processes that underpin decision-making. Much like a tree that draws its strength from its roots, the quality of a leader's decisions is heavily reliant on their underlying mental processes.

If you are seeking to make high-quality decisions, this is the book for you. Decision-making refers to the mental processes, conscious or unconscious, of choosing a course of action from a set of options. With remarkable strides in neuroscience in recent decades, we now have a better grasp of the workings of the human brain and nervous system. This book takes you on a journey to unravel the hidden layers of decision-making as seen through the lens of neuroscience. Following an introduction in the current chapter, Chapter 2 guides you through the life course of power – how a desire for power assists you in making decisions that help you rise to power but also, once in power, undermines the quality of decisions that can lead to your downfall. Chapter 3 dispels the misconception that emotions are adversaries of sound judgment. Instead, we explore how emotions can serve as valuable compasses to guide your decision-making. Moving to Chapter 4, we will learn about the workings of the dopaminergic system and how to harness it to make decisions that effectively motivate people. Next, Chapter 5 sheds light on how attention influences your decisions, and Chapter 6 explores the impact of memory on decision-making. Chapter 7 centers on the neuroscience underpinning trust, the glue that binds social relationships together. In Chapter 8, we discuss the powerful role of human faces, brimming with social and emotional cues, in shaping your decisions. Chapter 9 probes into where your personality comes from and its sway over your decision-making processes. Chapter 10 ventures into intuitive decision-making and gut feelings. Chapter 11 uncovers how mental shortcuts can lead to decision errors. And Chapter 12 is about brain-to-brain synchronization in collective decisions. The concluding chapter offers guidance on how to take care of our brains to make better decisions. The aim of this book is to equip leaders and those aspiring to lead with neuroscience insights and tools to make high-quality decisions. By the end of this book, you will find that exploring neuroscience and leaders' decision-making is one of the most rewarding decisions you will ever make. Are you ready to start this journey?

OUR BRAIN'S MOST IMPORTANT JOB

At the beginning of the journey, it is crucial to understand the fundamental role of the human brain. This understanding lays the foundation for the rest of the book, as we learn why our brains operate the way they do and how they influence our decision-making processes. First and foremost, what is our brain's most important job? While thinking, feeling, imagining, and creating are all important functions, they ultimately serve a grander purpose. The primary mission of our brains, and indeed all brains across species, is survival, ensuring that we pass on our genes to the next generation. We may choose not to have offspring, but that is a strategic decision rather than the primary mission of our brains.

Our brains oversee approximately 86 billion neurons, which are the nerve cells that form the foundational infrastructure of our nervous system. Collectively, they perform a vast array of operations, including supervising over 600 muscles for precise movement coordination, regulating dozens of hormone productions, powering the circulation of around 2,000 gallons of blood daily, and enabling our thoughts, creativity, and learning abilities.

Yet, despite their crucial role, our brains operate within a rather stringent energy budget. To survive, our brains have to optimize energy efficiency. This is like how leaders, who have finite resources, maximize efficiency within their organizations while facing constraints such as budget, time, and personnel. Picture it as a small department within your organization, constituting only 2% of the total organizational structure but consuming 20% of the resources (Raichle & Gusnard, 2002). Similarly, our brains account for 2% of our body weight but require approximately 20% of the blood supplied by a vast network of 600 kilometers of blood vessels (Kuzawa et al., 2014). Those blood vessels, including arteries, veins, and capillaries, ensure the delivery of vital resources such as oxygen and glucose to neurons, which are essential for their survival (Gailliot et al., 2007; Özugur et al., 2020). Our brains receive approximately 750–1,000 milliliters (0.75–1 liter) of blood per minute to support complex brain functions.

Due to its high metabolic cost, the brain is highly sensitive to the energy supply carried by the blood. When oxygen is lost for as little as 5 minutes, the death of neurons becomes almost irreversible (Magistretti & Allaman, 2015). If blood flow is not restored promptly, it can lead to brain death. In situations where the blood supply is limited, the brain takes top priority for its survival. For example, when we are under stress, our body's stress response is activated, causing physiological changes such as increased heart rate, rapid breathing, and elevated levels of stress hormones like cortisol to increase blood flow to our brains. Even if other organs need blood, our body attempts to supply the brain with a constant flow of blood. Saying yes to something means saying no to something else, and resources are allocated accordingly.

To optimize energy use, our brains, which are essential organs for decision-making, operate as energy-efficient prediction organs. How our brains make decisions is similar to how leaders make decisions, because a significant part of what leaders do is make decisions under uncertainty, which necessitates predictions. In our brains, to reduce uncertainty, the brain constantly processes sensory data such as images, sounds, and language and makes predictions based on past experiences to minimize the need for intense computational processing and conserve energy. When something unexpected arises, our brains have a stronger response (Heilbron et al., 2022). This is because unexpected events signal a prediction error, indicating that our brains' prediction model is inaccurate. To correct the prediction error, our brains have to update their prediction model, which requires additional computational resources and, hence, more energy. Imagine if we could travel back in time and change our past experiences – the changes would influence our brain's predictions, potentially leading to different decisions and behaviors. We do have the power to influence our future predictions. By learning new ideas, learning from people who disagree with us, and engaging in new activities, we can influence our brain's future predictions. This adaptability allows us to change our behaviors and perspectives over time.

A BRIEF TOUR OF THE HUMAN BRAIN

After understanding the most important job of our brains, let us take a brief tour of this decision-making organ. Consider our brains as a thriving metropolitan city with a mission to survive and thrive. In this brain city, approximately 86 billion neurons serve as diverse residents. Their job is to receive, evaluate, and transmit information to the next neuron. Each neuron, similar to city residents, has a specialized role. Some neurons are charged with processing sensory information, enabling us to perceive the world through sight, hearing, taste, smell, and touch. Other neurons are responsible for motor control, coordinating muscle movements, and facilitating actions. They function as the city's workforce, driving the execution of various tasks and activities. While each neuron plays its role as an individual resident, it is their collective effort and communication that give rise to the remarkable capabilities of processing information, generating thoughts and emotions, and carrying out intricate cognitive functions.

The communication between neurons is constant. Neurons communicate via electrical impulses and chemical signals known as neurotransmitters. Among more than 100 neurotransmitters in human brains, several of them are closely related to leadership: oxytocin is associated with trust (Kosfeld et al., 2005), dopamine is associated with motivation and obtaining a leadership position (Li et al., 2012, 2015) and serotonin is associated with human reactions to being treated unfairly (Crockett, 2009). The neurotransmitters are like couriers of the brain city. They navigate through intricate brain networks and cross synapses – the junctions between neurons – just as couriers navigate intersections within the city. They deliver vital messages and signals from one neuron to the next. Much like couriers carrying different types of packages from one place to another, different neurotransmitters carry specific signals or messages between neurons. For example, dopamine acts as a courier for reward and motivation signals, serotonin acts as a courier for mood regulation and glutamate acts as a courier for excitatory signals important for learning and memory. The neurotransmitters relay information related to sensory perception, memory formation, emotion regulation, and decision-making. Fueling these activities, as mentioned earlier, is a vast network of blood vessels that supply the energy-intense brain with necessary resources like glucose and oxygen.

Due to the brain's high energy demands, while accuracy in decision-making is essential, survival often takes precedence over absolute precision in the brain city. It recognizes the need for quick responses to potential dangers, much like a city's emergency services prioritize rapid action during crises. This prioritization of speed and efficiency over absolute accuracy enables the brain to make fast decisions, even if they are not always perfectly accurate. In the following chapters, we will revisit the brain's principle of energy optimization and its influence on our decision-making processes.

HUMAN BRAINS IN ORGANIZATIONS

In neuroscience, structure and function are inextricably linked. Brain regions are connected both structurally through neuroanatomical wiring and functionally through shared responsibilities. This interconnectedness means that one brain region supports numerous functions, and one function engages multiple brain regions (Gazzaniga et al., 2014). The same mechanism applies to organizations. The structure and function of the human brain bear many similarities to organizational structure and function. Brain regions can be likened to teams or departments within an organization, each with specialized functions and responsibilities. Different brain regions collaborate to process and interpret sensory information, perform specific tasks, and coordinate overall brain function, much like how different teams within an organization work together to achieve a shared goal. Neurotransmitters facilitate communication between neurons, allowing for the exchange of information and coordination of actions, resembling communication channels within an organization, such as face-to-face conversations, phone calls, and emails. Neurotransmitters also regulate and modulate neuronal activity, ensuring optimal brain function. Similarly, effective communication and information exchange are essential for smooth organizational functioning, impacting members' motivation, trust, and overall effectiveness.

Brain systems are akin to cross-functional teams in an organization. Just as different brain systems (e.g., attentional, memory, and emotional systems) work together to perform complex tasks and achieve overall brain functions, cross-functional teams bring together members from different departments or functional areas to work together on a specific project, leveraging their unique skills and expertise to achieve a shared goal. In the same way that our brains optimize energy to make decisions, leaders must optimize their resources – both human and material – to make the best decisions for their organizations. Different brain systems interact with one another, which then takes a winner-takes-all approach to generate a decision and sends motor commands to muscles to execute that decision (Gandhi & Katnani, 2011). This is why, despite numerous brain systems at work, we feel unified when making decisions. The brain operates as a unified entity, with all the systems working together as a whole.

Moreover, neurons do not function as simple on/off switches in a fixed wiring diagram. Instead, neurons respond in a continuous manner, adjusting their activity based on the intensity and pattern of incoming signals or stimulation. This adaptability of neuronal activity is at the core of brain plasticity, which refers to the brain's remarkable ability to reorganize its structure and modify its function in response to experiences, learning, and environmental changes. Similar to how individual neurons can modify their connections and adapt their activity, organizations also exhibit a similar level of plasticity in their structure and function. Much like the strength and efficacy of synaptic connections can be enhanced or weakened through experience, organizations can undergo structural changes that shape their operations and performance. In response to evolving external conditions (e.g., market changes, mergers, and acquisitions) or internal strategic shifts (e.g., adopting new technologies into operations), organizations experience changes in their functional teams. Through the process of restructuring or realigning, the teams adapt their roles and responsibilities to better align with organizational goals. This organizational restructuring can lead to improved specialization, more effective resource allocation, and newly established communication pathways, resembling the modifications in brain regions and their connectivity. With a foundational understanding of the similarities between our brains and organizations, we are now ready to explore the life course of power in leaders' decision-making.

2

THE LIFE COURSE OF POWER IN LEADERS' DECISION-MAKING

In social life, power is ubiquitous. It refers to having discretion and the means to asymmetrically exert influence over others' thoughts, decisions, and behaviors (Sturm & Antonakis, 2015). For leaders, such as a department head, power can be exercised through resource allocation, like budget and personnel, to influence subordinates' behaviors. The department head can reward employees who follow her directives with promotions, bonuses, or favorable assignments while punishing those who do not comply by demoting them or withholding resources. At times, the department head may adopt bullying tactics to exercise power, including intimidating, manipulating, belittling, and threatening employees who do not bow to her will. Bullies in the workplace, like bullies in other social settings, often target those who are perceived as weaker or more vulnerable because it is easier for bullies to exert control and influence.

Beyond the power derived from positions of authority, power can also be exercised through influencing tactics such as charm, ridicule, social exclusion, guilt-tripping, and spreading rumors. In parent–child relationships, children can make parents feel powerless, even though parents control critical resources for their children, including food, safety, emotional nourishment, and making most decisions on their behalf (Bugental & Lewis, 1999). Children can throw tantrums, pit parents against each other (e.g., telling mom that dad said "I can do it"), give parents silent treatment, and make parents feel guilty for resisting their child's demands (often through phrases like "If you love me, you would. . ."). Similarly, many workplace bullies do not hold positions of power, but they use similar influencing tactics to manipulate others' feelings, thoughts, and behaviors.

Power plays a critical role in leadership, a process wherein leaders influence others' behaviors to achieve a shared goal. Power can be used for the greater good, as exemplified by Abraham Lincoln's use of his presidential power to issue the Emancipation Proclamation. Power can also be used to enforce unyielding obedience, leading to power abuse, as demonstrated by authoritarians who use power to establish a repressive regime and suppress opposition. One can argue that an essential aspect of leadership is how to acquire power and decide when, where, to whom, and how it should be exercised. In this chapter, we embark on a journey through the life course of power and its influence on leaders' decision-making.

RISE TO POWER: UNVEILING THE DRIVING FORCES

What factors contribute to an individual's rise to power? A frequently examined trait is implicit power motive, also known as need for power or *n* Power. It is an innate, *unconscious* desire to influence others and control situations (Winter, 1973). This basic human need for control and influence is rooted in our evolutionary history, where having power and control often meant survival (Lammers et al., 2016). Not everyone has the same level of desire for power. You have probably encountered people with a voracious appetite for power – those who have an intense need for power, revel in the pursuit of control and dominance, believe themselves superior in intellect, and feel entitled to make decisions on others' behalf. People with a high power motive are driven by a need for social status and prestige, and they seek to attain positions of authority in order to gain control over others. Typically, they are confident, assertive, and ambitious. They often have decreased awareness of constraints, are willing to take risks, and feel invincible (Anderson & Galinsky, 2006; Whitson et al., 2013). They vie for leadership roles, compete for status and recognition, or exert influence over others in social settings.

The power motive is shaped by multiple factors in our neurobiology, one of which is the brain's dopaminergic reward system (Schultheiss & Schiepe-Tiska, 2013). This system governs our responses to rewards, fueling our pleasure-seeking behaviors and playing an integral role in reward-motivated behavior. The dopaminergic system starts in the ventral tegmental area (VTA), a region rich in dopamine neurons that produce the neurotransmitter dopamine (Chinta & Andersen, 2005). The VTA sends signals to the ventral striatum when activated by pleasure-associated stimuli, such as food (Demos et al., 2011) or music (Salimpoor et al., 2013). A key function of the dopaminergic system, particularly the VTA-to-ventral striatum pathway, is to encode reward prediction error – the difference between an *expected* reward and an *actual* reward received (Schultz, 2016). When the outcome of power-seeking behaviors – like competing for leadership positions, seeking to control resources, using aggressive tactics, or manipulating others – exceeds expectations, a positive prediction error is registered. This triggers a surge in dopaminergic activity, stimulating people with increased energy, vigor, and effort to engage in their goal-directed behavior (Kruglanski et al., 2012). When we feel powerful, we experience heightened levels of excitement, inspiration, joy, optimism, confidence, and euphoria, all of which propel us forward in pursuit of our goals (Anderson & Galinsky, 2006; Guinote, 2007).

This is why ascending the ranks of an organizational hierarchy invigorates and motivates people, triggering a dopamine surge that brings about a feeling of gratification. People with high power motives relish the opportunity to persuade and exert social influence (Spangler et al., 2014). They find pleasure in controlling others' behaviors through reward and punishment. They enjoy being a commanding figure and calling shots. Most presidential candidates want to be the US president not for financial gain but for power and status.

In fact, power motives are not exclusive to humans. The term "pecking order" originates from social hierarchies among chickens who establish their social hierarchy through pecking – a dominant chicken pecks subordinate ones without fear of retaliation, while those lower in the pecking order would not dare to return the peck. Similarly, monkeys assert dominance hierarchies in their groups through body language (e.g., standing upright, making direct eye contact with subordinates, and performing exaggerated movements such as chest-beating or shaking branches) and aggressive behaviors (e.g., fighting, biting, hitting, and threatening gestures like lunging or grabbing). When housed individually, monkeys have similar levels of dopamine. However, when placed in groups, hierarchies emerged, with dominant monkeys showing increased levels of dopamine, energy, and vigor (Morgan et al., 2002). This neurobiological mechanism explains why most people aim to climb an organizational ladder, but very few are willing to move downward in the hierarchy (Mitchell et al., 2020).

Some people have higher power motives than others. The hormone testosterone has been linked to power motive and dominance behavior. In men, testosterone is primarily produced in the testes – hence the name "testosterone." In women, testosterone is primarily produced in the ovaries and adrenal glands, albeit in smaller amounts. Once produced, testosterone circulates throughout the body via the bloodstream, influencing different cells and organs and regulating different bodily processes. While women do produce testosterone, the amount of testosterone that is present in men's blood plasma – a yellowish component of the blood that carries hormones, nutrients, oxygen, carbon dioxide, ions, and proteins – is seven to eight times higher than that of women.

Aside from its reproductive function, testosterone plays a crucial role in social behavior. Despite men having higher testosterone levels, the hormone's impact on social dominance is similar when accounting for gender-related differences (Grant & France, 2001). Testosterone has been associated with power motive (Schultheiss et al., 2005) and a range of power-related social behaviors, such as seeking out positions of power and leadership (van der Meij et al., 2016), competitiveness (Booth et al., 1989), entrepreneurial risk-taking (White et al., 2006), aggression (Archer, 2006), stress response (Dekkers et al., 2019), and occupational achievement (Dabbs, 1992). All of them can be advantageous for someone in a leadership role and make leadership roles more appealing to people with higher testosterone levels. Recall the chickens' pecking order. It was found that chickens' status increased along with testosterone levels (Allee et al., 1939). In humans, what happens when two team members both have high levels of testosterone? They compete for dominance and social status, which can create a highly competitive environment. Instead of collaborating toward the team's goals, they prioritize establishing their dominance, even if it comes at the expense of the team's collective goal.

Power serves leaders' decision-making in a favorable way. It makes leaders decisive. To speed up the decision-making process, powerholders' hearts pump faster and more forcefully, leading to increased blood circulation (Scheepers et al., 2012). The elevated circulation supplies more energy, which assists in decision-making and the ensuing behavior. Power boosts cognitive flexibility – the ability to respond to environmental inputs in a flexible manner. Power also boosts creativity. For example, powerful people come up with more novel product names compared to their less powerful counterparts (Gervais et al., 2013).

In general, powerholders' thought processes are less effortful, less deliberate, and consume fewer cognitive resources, but they are more flexible and more reliant on mental shortcuts. These mental processes underscore the profound impact of power on cognitive functions, perception formation, and decision-making. Importantly, power changes the very way powerholders view themselves and others (Chen et al., 2001). But power, if not used wisely, can be a slippery slope.

THE PERILOUS DESCENT: TRAPPED IN THE TOXIC POWER

People who assume positions of power often exhibit diminished empathy and compassion. They tend to demonstrate antisocial behaviors such as aggression, coercion, impulsiveness, and deceit. This phenomenon is known as the "power paradox," where the social and emotional skills most vital to leadership are the very abilities that degrade once people have power. The power paradox arises from excessive or constant activation of the dopaminergic reward system – a part of the brain that is associated with reward-motivated behavior – which can lead to addictive or impulsive behaviors detrimental to leaders and those they lead. Power is both intoxicating and addictive. The more power we have, the more we crave it. This is also why power has a tendency toward centralization. The lust for power can be a potentially dangerous craving, leading to abuse and a disregard for others' well-being. John Adams encapsulated this concern by stating, "The love of power is insatiable and uncontrollable. … There is danger from all men. The only maxim of a free government ought to be to trust no man living with power to endanger the public liberty" (Adams, 1772, para. 25). Adams' statement may seem like a cynical view of human nature, but it underscores the need for self-awareness of our own implicit power motives and an understanding of the life course of power in leaders' decision-making.

Power changes how the brain processes information and makes decisions in many ways. First, power influences our attentional system by narrowing our attention breadth (Willis et al., 2011), which enables us to have better working memory and clarity of focus, as well as achieve our goals without distraction (Harada et al., 2013). However, an overly narrow focus of attention means that we shift attention from others to ourselves (Willis et al., 2011). Due to the brain's high energy demand, we have a limited supply of attention as a cognitive resource. When we pay attention to one thing, we cannot pay attention to another. Power makes us pay more selective attention to our own desires, pursue personal rather than collective goals (Smith & Trope, 2006; Whitson et al., 2013), have an inflated sense of self and entitlement (van Kleef et al., 2015), and make self-serving decisions (Giurge et al., 2021). This is the mental underpinning of Lord Acton's aphorism, "Power corrupts, and absolute power corrupts absolutely" (Acton, 1887/1997, pp. 335–36).

In addition to the attentional system, power influences our memory, giving rise to three self-serving memory errors: forgetting negative events, fabricating false memories of positive events, and distorting negative memories into positive ones (Chew et al., 2020). Such memory errors make leaders falsely attribute success to their own abilities and take credit for a group's collective efforts, even if the success is by chance or unrelated to the leaders' decisions (Bénabou & Tirole, 2002). Moreover, memory errors activate a feeling of increased control over the course of events and disregard or underestimate the role of chance or external factors. This can lead to a distorted perception of their own competence, leading to overconfidence and hubris (Vitanova, 2021). This is why it is difficult for leaders to stay humble because it takes more brain energy to counteract the brain's automatic processes. Overconfidence and hubris are self-destructive and harmful to organizations.

The third way that power undermines leaders' decision-making is that power makes leaders discount others' advice. Leaders should listen and stay open-minded, but power makes people close their minds and become resistant to constructive criticism. As people move up the social hierarchical ladder, they take less advice from others (Tost et al., 2012) and conform less to others' opinions (Galinsky et al., 2008). Listening tours become more about ritualistic practices than opportunities for active listening. People in positions of power often override committees' recommendations, which undermines procedural justice, even though they have the authority to do so. Authoritarians make poor decisions, not only because of a lack of accurate information but also because they refuse to heed information that does not align with their preferences and expectations.

Fourth, power diminishes the ability to recognize the emotions of others (Nissan et al., 2015). Empathy, compassion, and gratitude are key elements that drive behaviors of sharing, cooperation, and altruism, contributing to one's enduring power. However, when those emotions wane and self-serving impulses take over, powerful people may increasingly become uncivil, disrespectful, and rude. Those behaviors can undermine trust and disrupt the very foundation of leadership – motivating people to achieve a shared goal.

Fifth, power makes leaders more decisive, often compromising accuracy in decision-making processes. There is a tradeoff between speed and accuracy. To make decisions quickly, leaders do not have enough time for careful deliberation to weigh the pros and cons. Instead, they tend to trust their gut feelings and rely on personal and temporary subjective experiences and stereotypes (Schmid & Amodio, 2017). Not only is the tendency to rely on those mental shortcuts amplified by experiencing power, but the amplifying effect can last more than a week (Weick & Guinote, 2008).

Sixth, power impairs self-control, leading people to prioritize their own interests at the expense of others and social norms. This manifests in impulsive and unethical behaviors such as interrupting others, committing grave policy violations, and breaching established norms and regulations. Notable examples include police officers being lectured at traffic stops by drivers who are in positions of power and Transportation Security Administration agents being confronted with the phrase, "Do you know who I am?" (Piff et al., 2012). In fact, experiences of power and privilege can make people behave like a form of psychological "brain damage" (Hogeveen et al., 2014). The concept of "acquired sociopathy" refers to a type of brain trauma typically incurred through a severe accident, such as a car crash or a fall. This trauma can damage the frontal lobes, brain regions responsible for empathy and active consideration of others. Such damage can drastically change a person's behavior, potentially turning kind and compassionate individuals into sociopaths – people driven by purely self-serving impulses. We are more likely to see an enraged boss than an angry subordinate. The diminished self-control also leaves an open door for powerholders' self-serving behavior, causing the moral compasses to go awry (Giurge et al., 2021). When feeling powerful, people are more likely to deem tax evasion acceptable or find no fault in over-reporting travel expenses or speeding on highways.

Recall the definition of power: having the discretion and means to asymmetrically exert influence over others, to control or direct their thoughts, behaviors, or decisions (Sturm & Antonakis, 2015). The life course of power in leaders' decision-making is marked by crests and troughs that encapsulate a paradox. Leaders are supposed to serve others by paying more attention to others than themselves, but the acquisition of power makes people shift valuable attention to themselves. Leaders are supposed to unite with others, but having power creates memory errors, which leads to arrogant narratives of their own superiority. Leaders are supposed to listen to others' input, but power makes people dismiss others' advice. Leaders are supposed to recognize the emotions of others and resonate with them, but power decreases people's ability to recognize emotions. Leaders are supposed to be deliberate and strategic, but power makes people rely on their gut feelings, subjective experiences, and stereotypes. Leaders are supposed to motivate a group of people to achieve a collective goal, but power impairs people's self-control, making them prioritize their own interests at the expense of others and societal norms. While power is often a necessary aspect of leadership, it can become addictive and toxic if mishandled. Understanding the life course of power is critical, as an imbalance in the use of power can lead to a leader's downfall. It is a fine line that requires continuous reflection, awareness, and balance to ensure that power serves as an enabler of positive leadership rather than a destructive force. History has taught us that powerful people rise and fall, and no one in this world has stayed in power forever.

3

EMOTION IS NOT AN ENEMY OF GOOD JUDGMENT

Leaders have frequently been advised not to let their emotions cloud their judgment. However, is it true that emotions interfere with sound decision-making? In this chapter, we will learn what an emotion is, what emotion is for, and why a clear dichotomy between emotion and rationality does not exist. Throughout this chapter, I will show how emotion can make or break leadership and how to look at leaders' decision-making through an emotional lens.

DEFINE EMOTIONS

Emotions are complex psychological and physiological responses that significantly influence our decision-making and behaviors. Feeling optimistic and hopeful, we are motivated to pursue innovative tasks, whereas feelings of apprehension make us more risk-averse in our decisions. These emotional responses are deeply interconnected with what we often refer to as "feelings," which are subjectively accessible states of our awareness or inner sensations known only to us (Damasio & Carvalho, 2013; De Waal, 2019). You may feel frustrated when team members fail to meet your expectations. Feelings of anger may arise when you are treated unfairly (Decety & Yoder, 2017; Sanfey et al., 2003). In contrast, emotions are frequently observable through a variety of physiological responses (e.g., blushing and elevated blood pression) and behavioral responses (e.g., facial expressions, body language, and vocal inflection). For example, a leader's pride can be perceptible to team members through upright and expansive posture, steady eye contact, and a clear, assertive tone of voice. Conversely, signs of stress or anxiety can be evident through fidgeting, avoiding eye contact, or a hesitant speech pattern.

FUNCTIONS OF EMOTIONS

Emotions often have observable manifestations that go beyond mere subjective experience, making them powerful tools for communication (Keltner & Haidt, 1999). These manifestations, such as facial expressions, body language, and tone of voice, serve as nonverbal cues for communication. Forty-two small muscles on each side of our faces make facial expressions to broadcast our emotional experiences to our social partners (Barrett, 2017; Ekman, 1993). People often say that your emotions are "written all over your face." That is because our facial expressions are the primary means by which we express emotions. In addition to faces, our body posture also conveys emotions. Expansive postures, where we stand erect and open up, are associated with emotions such as joy and awe (van Cappellen et al., 2022). Tone of voice is another significant aspect of how emotions are communicated nonverbally. While facial expressions and body language are powerful visual indicators, tone of voice provides an auditory signal that carries emotional weight. Vocal elements like pitch, pace, volume, and intonation can convey a range of emotions – enthusiasm can be expressed through a higher pitch and faster pace, while disappointment might be indicated by a slower pace and lower pitch (De Gelder & Vroomen, 2000). A calm and steady tone can evoke a sense of stability and reassurance among team members during turbulent times, while a tense or sharp tone may signal stress or dissatisfaction, alerting team members that something is amiss. In acting, actors and actresses use those observable manifestations to express the emotions of the characters they portray. This intentional display allows audiences to empathize with fictional characters, feeling joy, sorrow, fear, or excitement right along with them. The effectiveness of an actor or actress often hinges on their ability to authentically communicate these emotional states, enabling the viewer to emotionally invest in the story.

Now, consider the workplace. Imagine interacting with a leader who maintains a stoic facade, showing no emotional cues whatsoever. The absence of observable emotions can create a communication vacuum, making it difficult for team members to gauge the leader's thoughts or feelings. This lack of emotional display may result in an atmosphere of uncertainty and could hinder the formation of trust and social cohesion within the team. On the other hand, a leader who effectively communicates emotions – be it excitement about a new project, anger over unfair treatment, or gratitude for a job well done – creates an environment where team members feel seen, heard, and emotionally engaged.

In addition to their role in communication, emotions serve as drivers of motivation. Derived from the Latin word "emovere," where "e-" means "out" and "movere" means "move," the term "emotion" underlines its essential role as a motivator that propels us into action (Johnston & Olson, 2015). Political candidates often capitalize on emotions' motivation function by focusing on emotionally charged topics such as health care and immigration. These issues elicit strong emotional responses because they directly impact voters' lives. By evoking strong emotions, candidates can motivate citizens to act – particularly to vote. By contrast, other essential issues like agriculture, while important to national welfare, generally do not incite the same level of emotional engagement and, therefore, may not be as highly prioritized in public discourse. In corporations, when facing a market downturn, the emotion of fear can "move" a leader to take immediate defensive actions. After successfully completing a major project, a leader's feeling of gratitude can "move" and encourage them to nurture stronger social bonds within the team (Boyatzis et al., 2012).

More importantly, the motivational function of emotions is not intentional or deliberate but often automatic, acting as an intuitive guide for our behavior. Emotions quickly interpret a situation and automatically "move" us in a direction that has been evolutionarily programmed to be adaptive (Johnston & Olson, 2015). Our emotions are aroused *faster* than our thinking brains. It takes as little as 100 milliseconds (a tenth of a second) for our brain to produce an emotion, but it takes longer for the thinking part of our brain to catch up (Decety & Cacioppo, 2012). In essence, emotional responses precede cognitive deliberation. This is particularly beneficial in situations that require immediate action, where the time and cognitive resources needed for thorough analysis would be impractical. By facilitating quicker responses, emotional processing can help conserve cognitive resources, which are metabolically costly for the brain to employ. The emotion of disgust serves as a compelling example of how emotions can automatically influence behavior. Our automatic response to disgust is a mechanism that protects us from potentially harmful substances or situations. We smell spoiled food or accidentally eat a moldy blueberry, and our immediate feeling of disgust will likely cause a series of physical reactions, such as wrinkling our nose and feeling nauseous. Wrinkling our nose limits the intake of potentially harmful particles through the nostrils, reducing the risk of inhaling dangerous substances. It is a form of closing off or limiting our interaction with a contaminant. Feeling nauseous is a precursor to vomiting, which is a mechanism to eject ingested toxins from the body. These automatic responses serve as safeguards, compelling us to distance ourselves from the source of contamination – perhaps by promptly spitting out the moldy blueberry and taking steps to remove the spoiled food. Disgust extends beyond immediate sensory experiences like taste and smell. It can also manifest in social and moral contexts, such as a betrayal by a trusted friend or a leader who violates social norms and trust. If a policy proposal seems "fishy" or ethically unsound, the emotion of disgust may automatically prompt us to pull away from the proposal, often before we have even fully articulated why. This automatic response can act as a quick, albeit crude, ethical barometer, guiding us to further scrutinize the situation before making a decision.

AFFECT HEURISTIC

Using emotions as mental shortcuts in decision-making is often referred to as the "affect heuristic" (Finucane et al., 2000). Affect is an umbrella term for feelings, emotions, mood, and emotion-related traits. Affect heuristic is an efficient way to navigate complex situations where exhaustive information gathering would be impractical or overly laborious. It allows us to rapidly assess the desirability or risk associated with particular options, based on our emotional reactions to those options.

More importantly, emotions influence our decision-making in a predictable way (Wang, 2021). When emotions such as gratitude, empathy, or awe rise within us, they activate specific neural pathways correlated with altruistic behavior (Kini et al., 2016; Mathur et al., 2010). We are propelled toward behaviors that confer benefits on others. Emotions like fear or pride have a distinct neurological impact that functions like a spotlight, narrowing our scope of attention and effectively inducing a form of tunnel vision. This phenomenon can be explained by the brain's pursuit of energy efficiency. Feeling fearful or prideful, we are compelled to lean more heavily on pre-existing knowledge rather than venturing into the acquisition of new information. This restricted perspective often results in a propensity to adhere to familiar options, as opposed to exploring alternatives that might require consulting external viewpoints or advice (Lerner et al., 2015).

Emotions such as gratitude and shame, on the other hand, can transform the neurological "tunnel vision" into what can be likened to a panoramic view. These emotions activate specific regions of the brain, notably the prefrontal cortex, which is instrumental in expanding our attentional focus and promoting information-seeking behavior (Öhman, 2005). It appears as though these particular emotional states serve as catalysts, prompting our cognitive mechanisms to venture beyond their customary boundaries in pursuit of novel insights and perspectives. As a result, when influenced by emotions like gratitude or shame, we are more inclined to expand our options through the active solicitation of external advice (Fredrickson & Branigan, 2005).

Furthermore, decisions driven by rapid emotional responses often occur at a subconscious level. When we attempt to articulate the rationale behind our decisions, we frequently offer *post hoc* justifications. For example, you are a leader who must quickly decide whether to invest in a new project or not. Upon hearing a compelling presentation, you immediately feel a sense of excitement and optimism, prompting a quick decision to go ahead with the investment. Later, when asked to explain the rationale behind this decision, you may cite an array of factors such as market research, growth potential, and alignment with company objectives. However, these explanations may be post hoc rationalizations; the real trigger for the decision was likely the initial emotional response of excitement and optimism. In this case, the rapid emotional response – feeling optimistic about the project – drove the decision at a subconscious level. Only afterward did the cognitive system kick in to generate plausible reasons for making that decision, essentially reverse-engineering a logical explanation for an emotionally driven choice (Greene et al., 2004).

Intriguingly, the post hoc rationalizations are constrained by what enters our conscious awareness; however, the true impetus for these decisions and feelings often precedes conscious thought and is rooted in nonconscious processes (Gazzaniga, 2011). Despite what we may like to believe, leaders often make decisions based on these emotional shortcuts rather than pure logic. While it is socially accepted to say our decisions are rational and thought-out, the truth is that emotions play a significant role in the decision-making process.

MISCONCEPTION OF EMOTION-RATIONALITY DICHOTOMY

The intricate relationship between emotion and rationality in decision-making is far from a simple dichotomy. If emotion and rationality are two separate, isolated systems, then shutting down the emotional system (such as in patients with brain damage due to injury or legion) would lead to decisions that are purely rational. However, the reality is quite the opposite. These patients often struggle to make even simple choices, such as deciding what to wear or eat and evaluating whether it is safe to cross the street when a car is approaching at a certain speed. The lack of emotional input undermines their ability to evaluate the relative values or importance of different options (Bechara, 2004; Hogeveen et al., 2014). The idea that emotion and rationality are two separate, isolated systems is outdated.

In fact, the brain's emotional and cognitive systems are interdependent, both structurally and functionally. Structurally speaking, the anatomical connection between the two systems is integral to the decision-making process. For example, the amygdala, often dubbed the "emotional center" of the brain, has direct neural pathways to the prefrontal cortex, which is generally associated with rational decision-making, planning, and self-control. This anatomical linkage ensures that emotional input is incorporated almost instantly into rational deliberations (Bernston et al., 2007). When a leader faces a crisis situation, the amygdala may initiate a stress response. However, the prefrontal cortex can quickly intervene, modulating the emotional output from the amygdala. This interplay allows the leader to maintain composure and make informed, rational decisions despite emotional stimuli.

Moreover, at the cellular level, the production of emotions starts with individual nerve cells known as neurons. These neurons communicate with each other via chemical messengers called neurotransmitters, such as serotonin, dopamine, and norepinephrine. Importantly, these neurotransmitters serve dual roles in both the emotional and cognitive systems within the brain. For example, elevated levels of serotonin – potentially induced by factors like exposure to natural sunlight or aerobic exercises like running and swimming – can influence decision-makers to be more risk-averse, favoring conservative approaches over risk-seeking, reckless options. Serotonin thus plays a role not just in regulating mood but also in shaping risk-related decision-making.

Similarly, dopamine is released when a leader experiences a "win," like closing a significant deal. This neurotransmitter promotes feelings of pleasure and reward, reinforcing the neural connections used in the decision-making process that led to the desirable outcome (Tabibnia et al., 2008). This process, known as neural plasticity, makes it more likely that the leader will employ similar strategies in future decision-making scenarios. Further, dopamine is also pivotal for cognitive functions critical to leadership, such as attention, problem-solving, and even executive functions like planning and impulse control. Specifically, dopamine modulates the brain's prefrontal cortex, the region responsible for these higher order cognitive functions. Elevated dopamine levels can enhance attention, making it easier for a leader to concentrate on tasks that require deep thought or rapid decision-making. It can also improve problem-solving abilities, allowing the leader to consider multiple angles of a situation and arrive at an informed decision more effectively.

Norepinephrine, another key neurotransmitter, is released under stress and prepares the body for rapid action. Elevated levels of norepinephrine can improve alertness and attention, assisting a leader in focusing on essential information for fast decision-making. However, this neurotransmitter can also induce a form of "tunnel vision," narrowing the breadth of attention and possibly causing the leader to miss broader implications or alternative solutions. Here again, we see the neurotransmitter serving both emotional and cognitive roles, underscoring the importance of emotions' impacts on decision-making.

When a leader is in a performance review meeting and receives critical feedback on a recent project, the brain's intricate systems are fully engaged in processing this information. The amygdala evaluates the emotional tone of the feedback. If the feedback is positive, the amygdala may signal other parts of the brain to release dopamine, contributing to feelings of satisfaction and validation. If the feedback is negative, the amygdala may initiate a stress response, releasing neurotransmitters like norepinephrine to heighten alertness. Operating almost in parallel, the prefrontal cortex engages in logical analysis. It considers the facts presented, the reliability of the source, and the potential implications of the feedback. Should new strategies be adopted? Should the team's approach be revised? These are the types of questions the prefrontal cortex grapples with. The insula, serving as a sort of "integration hub," brings the emotional response from the amygdala and the logical conclusions from the prefrontal cortex into conscious awareness. This helps the leader not only understand the feedback but also how they feel about it, enabling a more nuanced response.

In any given situation, numerous brain regions and circuits (i.e., interlinked neurons and brain regions) collaborate to produce an emotional response. The emotional system is intrinsically linked to the attentional system, the memory system, and the dopaminergic reward system in the brain. Attentional systems, guided by neurotransmitters like norepinephrine, help the leader focus on salient points of the feedback. The memory system, influenced by both emotional and cognitive input, stores this information for future use, shaping how similar situations will be appraised later. Meanwhile, the dopaminergic reward system, fueled by neurotransmitters like dopamine, gears up to direct subsequent behavior – whether that is seeking to replicate a positive outcome or avoid a negative one. In the case of a leader receiving critical feedback, the attentional system, guided by neurotransmitters, helps the leader focus on crucial aspects of the feedback. This allows for sifting through a potential mix of praise and criticism to identify actionable items. Emotional and factual elements of the feedback get stored for future reference (Keltner et al., 2014). The next time a similar project is undertaken, this stored information will likely influence how it is approached. Depending on the overall appraisal of the feedback – both emotional and rational – this system may either reinforce the current approach if the feedback is positive or adjust strategies for improvement if the feedback is negative.

Emotions are intrinsically woven into the fabric of decision-making processes (Thagard, 2012). To navigate the complex landscape of leadership, acknowledging, understanding, and leveraging emotions are not just advisable; they are essential. A leader's emotions can influence their attention, willingness to take risks, and overall approach to problem-solving. Meanwhile, being attuned to the emotional states of team members can help leaders gauge team morale, engagement, and motivation. Recognizing signs of stress, dissatisfaction, or enthusiasm among team members can inform managerial approaches – whether it is offering targeted support, modifying project goals, or capitalizing on collective enthusiasm to drive innovation.

4

MAKING DECISIONS TO MOTIVATE OTHERS

Leadership was adeptly described by former US President Dwight D. Eisenhower as "the art of getting someone else to do something you want done because he wants to do it" (Eisenhower, 1954, 0:05). Central to this description is "want," which is associated with motivation. Why are we motivated to do one thing but not another? Motivation can be seen as a series of cost–benefit valuations where we measure the effort required (the cost of an action) against the expected rewards (its benefits; Chong et al., 2016). In this chapter, we will explore the neural mechanisms associated with "want" and how leaders can leverage the brain's "want" mechanism to motivate others.

EMPOWERMENT

Power is a motivating force, as we have already learned in Chapter 2. Leaders who want to motivate others toward a shared goal need to empower them. Empowerment is defined as "increased intrinsic task motivation" (Thomas & Velthouse, 1990). When empowered, people's behavioral approach system (BAS), which is associated with the dopaminergic system that regulates behavior in response to rewards, is activated. Once activated, people are in a heightened state of motivation and have an amplified desire to pursue goals, take initiative, and engage in actions that can potentially lead to rewards or positive outcomes (Sutton & Davidson, 2000). In one study, compared to low-power participants, high-power participants had greater left frontal activation in the alpha band, which was a specific range of brainwave frequencies that indicated greater approach motivation (Amodio et al., 2004). This explains why power motivates people to approach and engage with rewarding stimuli. In another study, high-power participants were more likely to reposition an annoying fan in a room compared to low-power participants, suggesting that they were more likely to take action to achieve their desired results (Galinsky et al., 2003). If we want to motivate people, we give them power, control, and autonomy.

Conversely, lower power activates the behavioral inhibition system (BIS), which regulates behavior in response to potential threats and aversive stimuli. The BIS functions as an "alarm system" that is characterized by heightened vigilance and a focus on potential risks. People experiencing BIS activation tend to approach situations more cautiously, hesitating to take action until they have thoroughly evaluated the circumstances. Without empowerment, people tend to perceive their environment as more threatening and less rewarding than those with power.

As we learned in Chapter 2 about the life course of power in leaders' decision-making, power, while a potent motivator, can also be toxic and addictive. There must be checks and balances in place to prevent power holders from using their advantageous positions to satisfy their own interests rather than the interests of the group (Pratto, 2015). In organizations, there are many factors that are barriers to empowerment, ranging from organizational structure, organizational culture, job design, access to resources, employee rewards and ownership, employee traits and skills, autonomy, mutual trust, leader selection, and leaders as role models (Yukl & Becker, 2006). Leaders need to build a system that eliminates those constraining factors of empowerment.

GOAL-SETTING

What propels us forward, fuels our ambition, and shapes our direction? It is a goal – an aim of action (Latham & Locke, 1991). Leadership, at its core, is about motivating people to achieve a shared goal. A team without a goal is like a ship without a compass. Goals infuse the daily grind with purpose, challenge, and meaning. They are the fabric that weaves people into a cohesive unit, driven by a common purpose (i.e., a vision or mission).

Why do goals captivate our minds and drive our actions? Once we set a goal, our brains begin to allocate resources, such as attention, emotional, and dopaminergic systems, and align them with the desired outcome. Together, they direct our efforts toward achieving the goal. Goals focus our attention, which casts a spotlight on the tasks that are instrumental to achieving the goal. When goals resonate with our desires and ambitions, it forges a powerful emotional bond that fuels motivation, propelling us forward with increased motivation. Further, accomplishing a goal is inherently motivating because the dopaminergic system is associated with regulating goal-directed behavior. When we set and subsequently achieve a goal, the brain releases dopamine, a neurotransmitter associated with feelings of pleasure and reward reinforcement. The release of dopamine creates sensations of satisfaction and accomplishment. Essentially, our brain interprets goal achievement as a favorable outcome, signaling to us that our efforts have been fruitful. As a result, the release of dopamine creates a positive feedback loop that not only reinforces the behavior that led to goal attainment but also encourages us to pursue similar goals in the future (Schultz, 2016).

Not all goals have the same effect on motivation. Leaders must ensure that the goals are specific, challenging, and shared. First, specific goals are clear, leaving no room for ambiguity. Specific goals have a stronger effect on motivation than ambiguous goals such as "do your best." The problem with encouraging people to "do their best" lies in the lack of clarity and the absence of external referents for evaluation. Without specific landmarks, a team wanders aimlessly, akin to a ship adrift at sea without a compass. A specific goal, including timelines, functions as a clear roadmap, directing our focus and energy toward a well-defined outcome. Moreover, the visualization of reaching a well-defined goal activates the default mode network – a network of brain areas that show increased activity when the brain is at rest, such as during daydreaming and mind-wandering, and is disengaged from the external world. The term "default" aptly describes this network's baseline function. The default mode network is also active when we remember the past and envision the future. A vision articulated by a leader that galvanizes and inspires people activates people's default mode network. Unfortunately, many organizations' vision statements have a "blurry vision bias" – people's preference for abstract, nonvisual language that lacks clarity. To overcome the blurry vision bias and to make a vision inspiring and motivating, leaders must engage their team members' default mode network, taking them to mental time travel by activating their five sensory systems. This engagement can be achieved with vivid, sensory-driven rhetoric that paints a concrete picture of the future, letting them see, hear, smell, taste, and touch what lies ahead. It is this vicarious mental experience that ignites hope, sparks excitement, and triggers emotions that are not only motivational but also contagious.

Challenging but attainable goals ignite growth. When we set ambitious yet reachable goals, we pave the road to progress. The challenges invigorate our resilience and determination, transforming barriers into opportunities. However, caution is warranted here. Goals that are too ambitious or unrealistic, instead of motivating people, lead to frustration and demotivation. What is worse, unattainable goals create an unethical culture, particularly in a punitive environment. To avoid failing to meet goals and facing potential consequences, employees are tempted to manipulate outcomes (Park et al., 2022). An example is the Wells Fargo scandal, where employees created fake accounts to meet unrealistic sales goals (Williams, 2020).

The goal-setting process must be participatory. Teams with goals set through a participatory process performed better than those with assigned goals. A participative goal-setting process not only creates a shared goal but also makes it resonate with team members' personal values and aspirations. As a result, the shared goals provide a narrative that gives meaning to collective efforts, symbolizing shared values and a shared vision.

COOPERATION

Cooperation plays a critical role in the emergence and success of small groups, organizations, and societies. Cooperation refers to people pooling resources, sharing knowledge and skills toward a shared goal, or engaging in mutually beneficial interactions (Rand & Nowak, 2013). Notably, the definition of cooperation bears resemblance to that of leadership – the ability to influence, motivate, and guide others toward achieving a shared goal. Both cooperation and leadership require people to work together to achieve a shared goal. In that sense, understanding why people cooperate with others – or fail to do so – is of paramount importance for leaders. Cooperation becomes more complicated as groups get bigger. When groups grow beyond two people, it is not enough to focus only on individual behaviors. We need to keep track of everyone's cooperative behavior, or lack thereof, and how it collectively influences the process of achieving a shared goal. Before discussing how leaders can promote cooperation, let us look at what takes place in our brains when we decide to cooperate.

When we make decisions, our brain engages in a value-based process (Bartra et al., 2013). During this process, our brains evaluate different options based on potential outcomes or rewards, assigning a subjective value to each option. The subjective value reflects the perceived desirability of an option, considering not only the objective outcome but also personal preferences, goals, expectations, and contextual factors. For example, the same outcome

may hold varying values for different people depending on personal preferences or situational elements. For the subjective values of different options to
be comparable, they need to be converted into a universal neural code or
"common currency" (Levy & Glimcher, 2012). This process enables us to
compare and balance different values (e.g., personal gain vs societal benefit)
and select the option that is deemed most valuable to us, thereby guiding
goal-directed behavior. To simplify value computations, we can break them
down to three key parameters: outcomes, probabilities, and social preferences
(van Bavel et al., 2022). A wide range of mental processes provide information
on the three parameters, influencing our cooperative decisions. Now it is time
to look at how leaders can influence the three parameters – outcomes, probabilities, and social preferences – to promote cooperative behavior.

Make the Outcomes of Cooperation Attractive

Leaders must make the outcomes of cooperative behavior attractive. To do so,
leaders can develop a system that rewards cooperative behavior and punishes
behavior that deviates from cooperation (Gu€rerk et al., 2006). For example,
when policy changes either allow or disallow certain behaviors, they change
the possible outcomes associated with different choices. The brain's dopaminergic system is highly sensitive to positive reinforcement, influencing how we
perceive and react to rewards and punishments. When knowledge sharing is
acknowledged and rewarded, such as by public recognition, the brain's
dopaminergic system signals that sharing is more valuable than withholding
information, boosting our motivation to cooperate. The dopaminergic system
also interacts with the memory system, specifically a brain region called the
hippocampus, ensuring that attractive outcomes from cooperation are
remembered for future decision-making (Shadlen & Shohamy, 2016).

To further illustrate this point, consider a scenario where you and a
colleague named Adam are working on a group project. You put your heart
and soul into drafting the proposal, covering all details like budget, personnel,
timeline, and evaluation, while Adam only contributes to the project by
making a couple of minor edits to the proposal and submitting it to your
supervisor. The proposal is successful, but Adam never mentioned to anyone
that you were the one drafting it and doing the lion's share of the work.
Instead, Adam takes the credit and is even rewarded with a bonus for the
project's success. Would you collaborate with Adam again? Likely, the
negative experience would be stored in your hippocampus, and your brain's

dopaminergic system would caution against repeating the same cooperative behavior again.

Increase the Probabilities of Cooperation

To motivate cooperative behavior, leaders can also increase the probability of cooperation by establishing collaboration as part of group norms. Group norms are a set of shared expectations, beliefs, or standards of behavior that are commonly accepted and followed within a group. The group norms act as guidelines, indicating how others are likely to behave and thus shaping the probability of cooperation. A strong adherence to social norms suggests that we can expect others to behave in quite predictable ways (Gelfand, 2019). When cooperation is set as our group norm, we know that we are expected to cooperate, and our team members are expected to do so as well. If a behavior deviates from the group norm, the insula in our brains detects the change and adjusts our expectations accordingly (Gu et al., 2015). If leaders establish mechanisms for detecting and punishing noncooperative behavior, team members can conclude that their interaction partners are less likely to deviate from cooperation because they are disincentivized from taking advantage of other team members' cooperation (Zucker, 1986).

To create a cooperative group norm, leaders also need to reduce the probabilities of exploitation for cooperative team members, as seen in the free rider problem. This phenomenon, where people seek to benefit from others' contributions without contributing themselves, is detrimental to cooperation. One of the primary reasons for free riding is self-interest. People choose to free ride to maximize their own gains while minimizing their contribution to the public good (Andreoni, 1988). Leaders must be vigilant to enforce fairness, minimize the free-riding problem, and promote a fair and cooperative group norm.

Moreover, group norms can be reinforced through indirect reciprocity. Unlike direct reciprocity, where immediate benefit is expected, indirect reciprocity relies on reputation or past behavior (Panchanathan & Boyd, 2004). In groups, we choose to cooperate not necessarily because we expect a direct return from the person we are helping but because we trust that our cooperative behavior will be recognized and reciprocated by others in the future. The trust and expectation of future reciprocity can increase the probabilities of cooperation, strengthening the cooperative group norm (Rand et al., 2014).

Cultivate Positive Social Preference

The third way for leaders to motivate cooperative behavior is to cultivate positive social preference. Social preference – the degree to which decision-makers prioritize others' interests over their own – can significantly influence cooperation. Leaders often need to manage team members' different levels of social preference. Consider a high-stakes project with a tight deadline. Team members with high social preference actively engage in open communication, share information willingly, and contribute their skills and expertise in order to achieve the team's goals. They prioritize the project's success over personal ambitions or preferences and are willing to compromise and make sacrifices. By contrast, team members with low social preference prioritize personal gains, leading to a lack of synergy and reduced collaboration in the team. Variations in social preferences have been found to be associated with a brain area known as the temporoparietal junction (TPJ; Fehr & Camerer, 2007). The TPJ is responsible for understanding and interpreting team members' perspectives, emotions, and intentions. It allows us to put ourselves in others' shoes, which promotes empathy and facilitates effective collaboration (Parkinson et al., 2017). To safeguard the sustainability of cooperation and protect team members with high social preferences, leaders should consider separating team members based on their high or low social preferences. This practice guards against selfish individuals taking advantage of cooperative team members.

Leaders can also cultivate positive social preference by crafting a shared identity for their teams. People naturally exhibit a preference for in-group members who share similar characteristics while displaying hostility and aggression toward out-group members (van Bavel & Packer, 2021). A broadly defined shared identity is a fundamental element of cooperative decision-making. An example of a shared identity can be observed among astronauts aboard the International Space Station. Their shared identity is not delineated by their nationalities but rather emerges from their shared interests and experiences in a unique and challenging environment of space. Living and working in close quarters, astronauts depend on each other for support, thereby nurturing a profound sense of interdependence. Effective leaders are adept at crafting a shared identity to increase cooperation.

By changing the three parameters (outcomes, probability, and social preference) of how people compute subjective values of cooperation, leaders can lay the foundation for fruitful cooperation that propels their teams to achieve a shared goal. Motivating others is the most essential task of leaders. Through empowerment, goal-setting, and cooperation, leaders can transcend individual team member's interest and effort to achieve a shared goal.

5

"PAY" ATTENTION

In a crowded room filled with a cacophony of voices, laughter, and music, you engage in a conversation with a friend while filtering out the background noise. This remarkable ability, known as the "cocktail party effect," demonstrates how our brains prioritize and selectively process relevant information amid competing stimuli. In a world overflowing with data and demands, leaders are presented with a paradox: an abundance of information leads to a scarcity of a crucial resource – attention. Leaders grapple with challenges like information overload, frequent distractions, high stress levels, decision fatigue, and the need to balance short-term and long-term priorities. To address those challenges and optimize leaders' and team members' attention, it is important to understand how the brain's attention system works.

ATTENTION AS A SPOTLIGHT

The attentional system exists to tackle a unique predicament. Consider our brain as a bustling command center, ceaselessly bombarded with sensory information. Our brains are not like computers with upgradeable processors that can crank up the dial on information processing. Instead, the brain has a set processing capacity. This information processing limitation is called "mental bandwidth." It suggests that human cognitive capacity is roughly equivalent to processing 60 bits of information per second (Just & Carpenter, 1992). When the onslaught of information surpasses this capacity, our brains do not expand to accommodate it. Fortunately, our brains have a cognitive spotlight – the attentional system, which acts like a spotlight, selectively illuminating certain aspects of our environment. The focused beam represents our primary focus, vivid and clear, while elements outside the spotlight remain less defined yet within our peripheral awareness. Our attentional spotlight can shift around the stage of awareness, narrowing and widening its beam. As you read this passage, your attention narrows to each word while still maintaining a broader understanding of the text.

Imagine you are in a meeting with multiple team members, each of whom is providing an update on their respective tasks. While they are speaking, your brain processes their spoken words, their nonverbal cues, the implications of what they are saying, your responses, and potentially even thoughts about other unrelated matters. All of this information processing happens within your brain's limited processing capacity. Intriguingly, processing visual information reduces activity in auditory areas, meaning we expend less energy processing environmental sounds. It works the other way around as well: when we attend to auditory information, we reduce our visual processing activity. Consider that amidst this flurry of information, an unexpected interruption occurs, such as a phone call, a sudden question, or a burst of noise from outside the room. The influx of additional data strains your cognitive processing, possibly resulting in attention lapses or memory gaps because your "bandwidth" is already at capacity.

However, our attentional spotlight does not run on endless energy. Instead, our attention is budgeted like a cognitive currency. Our brains have to make calculated decisions about where to invest their cognitive currency (Raichle & Gusnard, 2002). It is this competitive allocation process that sets the stage for our interaction with the environment, determining what makes it into the spotlight of our attention. Whether we are navigating a complex decision-making process or orchestrating team dynamics, we need to effectively allocate our attention, minimize distractions, and promote a purposeful approach to information processing. Remember that it is not about processing more, it is about focusing our attention on what matters most. This point can be illustrated by Albert Einstein's witty observation: "Any man who can drive safely while kissing a pretty girl is simply not giving the kiss the attention it deserves." We are selective with our attention because we lack the mental capacity to process all the available information out there. Attention, by nature, is selective. We pay attention to one thing while simultaneously ignoring others. When we say "pay attention," we do "pay" for it – at a mental cost.

Our selective attention poses a biological constraint on our decision-making. We may take pride in our ability to multitask, but neuroscience evidence suggests a biological constraint on multitasking. Activities requiring selective attention cannot be performed simultaneously. When we attempt to multitask, we rapidly switch between tasks, resulting in subpar performance. In one experiment, researchers conducted four experiments where participants had to switch between different tasks or perform the same task repeatedly (Rubinstein et al., 2001). Switching between tasks was found to incur switching-time costs. It means that when participants switch tasks, they must first shift their goals and then activate the rules applicable to the new task. Consequently, it took participants longer to switch between tasks than to perform the same task repeatedly, especially when the rules were more complex. In addition to the switching-time costs, there is also a control cost, which is the difficulty in controlling transitions between different mental states in the brain (Kamiya et al., 2023). It is like navigating multiple mental lanes. The mental effort required to maintain control can lead to the dreaded mental fatigue we are all familiar with. This is why multitasking or switching between tasks frequently reduces efficiency and productivity. Multitasking is overrated. It is recommended that leaders minimize multitasking and focus on one task at a time to optimize performance and productivity.

WHAT CAPTURES ATTENTION?

In decision-making processes, attention has a profound influence on the evaluation and selection of options. The more attention given to certain options, the more likely they are to be chosen (Smith & Krajbich, 2018). Whether making strategic business decisions, resolving moral dilemmas, or cultivating a cooperative team environment, leaders can subtly influence decisions by directing attention to specific aspects and aligning decisions with organizational values and goals. Here is how neuroscience can help leaders attract others' attention.

Novelty

Our attention can be captured by anything that is new or unusual. The attraction to novelty is part of our survival instinct, which can be traced back to our ancestors, who were constantly on the lookout for new threats and opportunities in their environment. To re-engage people and regain their attention, leaders can introduce novel elements. Instead of a standard presentation, consider using an interactive digital tool, video, or game.

Novelty is associated with uncertainty. Uncertainty can be viewed as a form of cognitive or informational conflict that attracts our attention and motivates us to resolve it. When faced with uncertain or novel situations, our attentional system is activated to gather more information and reduce uncertainty. Uncertainty can attract attention in different ways. It can capture our attention by interrupting ongoing cognitive processes as unexpected or uncertain events draw our focus away from routine or predictable stimuli. Uncertainty can also enhance attention by increasing alertness and vigilance, preparing us to process and respond to new information. Additionally, uncertainty is closely related to salience, which is the degree to which a stimulus is prominent or important in capturing attention. Uncertain or unexpected stimuli tend to have high salience because they stand out and demand our attention. The brain's attentional system is attuned to detecting and prioritizing such salient stimuli. To leverage these cognitive mechanisms, leaders can consider disrupting routine patterns or presenting unexpected information.

Movement

Our attention is easily drawn to movement. Our propensity to gravitate toward movement is deeply rooted in our primal instincts. This inclination can be attributed to a survival mechanism for quickly detecting movement, which in ancient times could have indicated the presence of a potential predator or valuable prey. Our ancestors lived in a constant state of vigilance, as they needed to remain alert to both threats and opportunities for survival. As a result, as a survival mechanism, our attention has become inherently attuned to motion. This inclination toward movement, refined by extensive periods of adaptation, continues to influence our decision-making processes in the modern context. Leaders can use a hand gesture to direct the audience's attention to a specific area or object in order to emphasize its significance. This technique is particularly useful when discussing visual aids or highlighting key elements.

Attention diminished over time. After 15 minutes of inactivity, our attention begins to wane with the passage of time. This phenomenon is rooted in the brain's remarkable ability to adapt and refocus its attention. In the same way that a spotlight can be adjusted to illuminate specific areas, our brain adjusts its cognitive spotlight to focus on what it deems important. To keep people engaged and attentive during a lengthy meeting, leaders can change the setup halfway through, or simply standing and walking around while speaking can refocus the attention of attendees who may be losing concentration. In an online environment, interactive elements such as polls or quizzes can serve the same purpose. To capture their audience's attention during a discussion, leaders can also use hand gestures, body language, and position changes.

Intensity

Intensified stimuli have the inherent capability to capture our attention. The stimuli, characterized by their vibrant brightness, deafening loudness, startling touch, and other forms of pronounced intensity, command our attention. Imagine fireworks display at night. The brilliant burst of colors against the backdrop of darkness exemplifies vibrant brightness that captures our attention instantaneously. Fire hydrants and ambulances are often colored in shades of red, and this choice of color is not arbitrary. The vibrancy and intensity of the red hue attract attention and communicate urgency. Similarly, incorporating visually striking elements into a presentation or communication can effectively draw attention to key points. Leaders can use bold typography, italics, and vibrant colors to draw attention to crucial points. Use this technique sparingly to avoid overstimulation and mental fatigue.

Emergency sirens are an example of deafening loudness. Designed to be significantly louder than typical background noise (around 40–60 decibels), emergency sirens often reach 120 decibels or higher. This intensity serves two primary functions. First, the sheer volume of the siren ensures that it can be heard from a considerable distance, even in urban environments. Second, the intensity of the sound elicits a heightened physiological response, engaging the amygdala, which plays a central role in processing emotions and initiating the fight-or-flight response. Similarly, other loud sounds, such as thunder and primal screams, can quickly shift our attention to potential dangers, reflecting the brain's instinctive response to sudden and intense auditory cues. This insight can assist leaders in modifying vocal tone or volume to emphasize important information.

A sudden, intense touch, such as a tap on the shoulder, has the ability to jolt our attention. This tactile stimulus showcases the brain's sensitivity to pronounced intensity, making us instantly alert and engaged. The power of tactile stimuli can be used by leaders to direct attention and engage an audience. For example, leaders can establish a personal and engaging connection by placing a hand on someone's arm, especially when combined with eye contact. This can be used to emphasize empathy, sincerity, or the significance of a particular message. Leaders can also briefly pause and then lightly touch an object or a document to create a natural break in the conversation that draws attention to what is being touched. This can be effective for transitioning between topics or emphasizing particular details. However, the effective application of tactile cues requires a nuanced approach. Leaders must consider cultural norms, personal boundaries, and the appropriateness of physical interactions in different contexts. What is impactful and engaging for one audience may not have the same effect on another. As with any attention-capturing technique, moderation and sensitivity are essential for avoiding discomfort or overstimulation.

Contrast

Changes in the environment attract our attention. Our brains are wired to seek out elements that stand out from their surroundings. Distinct characteristics act as attention magnets, drawing our attention to what is unique. Dark text against a bright background, or vice versa, creates a stark contrast that draws attention to the text. Using color accents or highlights to emphasize specific words, phrases, or images can also effectively direct the reader's attention to critical information. Also attracting our attention are sudden changes in sound (e.g., a sound produced by a dropped object), light (e.g., flashing lights on emergency vehicles), and temperature (e.g., plunging into a cold pool on a hot day).

Leaders can use contrast as a strategic communication tool to capture people's attention. Using contrasting colors to highlight critical points in a presentation, for example, draws attention to those elements. A leader can also create an auditory contrast by slightly leaning in and lowering the volume while speaking. The change in tone draws the audience's attention to the message's intimate nature. This approach is particularly effective when communicating sensitive or important information because it creates a sense of connection and significance.

Emotion

Emotionally charged stimuli are effective attention-getters. Again, our brains are geared toward survival. Due to limited attention and processing capacity, we need to be selective with the information we use and find ways to process it efficiently. Emotions signal what we need to pay attention to, and we prioritize the emotions that influence our survival (Pratto & John, 1991). In Chapter 3, we learned that different emotions result in distinct decision outcomes. The way in which information is presented and the nature of the task can elicit different emotions and direct our attention to different facets of the available options, thereby influencing our decisions.

Relevance

Our attention is naturally drawn to what is relevant to our goals. Our brain's ability to direct attention is closely tied to our interests and goals. We allocate more cognitive resources to stimuli that align with our current goals or personal motivations. When delegating tasks, leaders have an opportunity to demonstrate how a task contributes to a team member's goal, the team's goals, and the organization's vision. This understanding transforms the task from a mere task assignment to a meaningful contribution, capturing team members' attention and boosting their motivation. Recognizing each team member's individual motivations is equally important. When leaders understand what motivates their team members, be it personal growth, recognition, or a sense of purpose, they are able to align tasks with these intrinsic motivators. Not only does the alignment boost engagement, but it also ensures that the team members remain invested in their work.

Social Cues

Humans are social creatures who pay attention to social cues. They include eye direction, facial expressions, body language, and tone of voice. These cues convey information about emotions and intentions, which is useful for decision-making. Human faces tend to attract more attention than other objects or texts, highlighting our innate preference for social interaction, which will be discussed in detail in Chapter 8.

Another social cue that commands our attention is power. How we allocate our precious attention is also influenced by power. Being in a position of power and feeling powerful enable powerholders to have a more positive self-perception and pay more attention to themselves. This psychological effect also makes powerholders pay diminished attention to others. People in positions of power are more likely to dismiss others' advice than those with less power. Powerful people also spent less time looking at their conversation partners. To counteract the detrimental effect of power on their decision-making, leaders should actively pay less attention to themselves and more attention to others. For example, if a leader observes a team member's facial expression indicating confusion or disagreement during a meeting, addressing the issue promptly can increase engagement and understanding. By paying attention to social cues, leaders are able to address concerns in real time, keeping the team on the same page and engaged.

Understanding how all of these signals naturally attract attention allows leaders to communicate more effectively and engage their team or audience. You can use novelty and emotions to highlight an important point or use relevance to ensure that your message is directly applicable to the listeners' interests or goals. You can also be more aware of these environmental signals, enabling you to make better decisions.

6

IF MY MEMORY SERVES

Memory's function is to retain and recall past experiences, knowledge, skills, and perceptions that are essential for daily functioning and adaptive behavior. Leaders rely on their memory to learn from past decisions, identify patterns, and adapt to new challenges. Without memory, we would be crippled in daily life and in leadership roles. It would be impossible to make decisions based on trial and error because we would not remember our previous mistakes. Likewise, leaders would struggle to recall past strategies, client interactions, or key decisions.

In contrast to the commonly held belief that memories are like photographs, we reconstruct memories to fit our perceptions and emotions. For example, memories of significant experiences like promotions and important global events like 9/11 are likely to be more vivid than memories of what you had for lunch three years ago. This phenomenon is known as the "availability heuristic," in which information that is more easily accessible in our memories has a greater influence than other information. This tendency renders leaders susceptible to making poor decisions because they rely solely on the vividness of memories.

Memory has three phases: encoding, storage, and retrieval (Klein, 2015). At the core of memory is a process called "encoding." This process converts the information we receive into a format that can be stored and retrieved later. This encoding process takes place at the cellular level, where the connections between brain cells are either strengthened or weakened, analogous to making certain paths in a forest easier or harder to navigate. When the connections between brain cells are reinforced, the information encoded in those cells becomes more accessible for storage and retrieval, similar to well-trodden forest paths. Simultaneously, other connections are weakened, causing the information encoded in those cells to become less prominent, akin to less traveled paths. Moreover, our brain cells produce proteins that facilitate the strengthening and weakening of neural connections, a fundamental process for encoding information effectively. Subsequently, during the storage phase, the encoded information is retained through various neural connections and structures over time. When retrieval occurs, the brain accesses and reactivates previously stored memories, bringing them to conscious awareness for decision-making. This intricate process demonstrates how the memory system does not function like a camera, encoding every detail that feeds into our sensory systems. Instead, it processes and stores information selectively, making memory fragile. Daniel L. Schacter categorized the major memory problems into seven "sins": transience, absent-mindedness, blocking, misattribution, suggestibility, bias, and persistence (Schacter, 2002).

SEVEN SINS OF MEMORY

Transience

Transience, or the gradual fading of memory over time, has far-reaching implications for leaders' decision-making. Memory fading is a carefully orchestrated process involving two brain systems: encoding and retrieval. Think of this process as an orchestra, where some instruments play louder tunes for certain memories, helping them linger, while others permit memories to gracefully exit the stage. Specifically, the left hemisphere is responsible for encoding verbal information, whereas the right hemisphere is in charge of nonverbal encoding. If we do not recall them frequently, our memories may fade away. Leaders should pay close attention during the encoding phase of critical information to ensure that vital details do not fade. For example, leaders often receive feedback from their team members, which provides valuable insights into workplace dynamics and opportunities for improvement. When making decisions about team management or organizational changes, a leader may overlook crucial details if they do not actively engage with the feedback or encode it correctly.

Absent-Mindedness

Absent-mindedness refers to shallow or distracted processing that results in weak memories or forgetting upcoming tasks. Consider misplacing your car keys or forgetting a child in the car. Memory lapses occur due to insufficient attention during the initial encoding phase (Burgess, 2000). This is a common reason we forget things. Leaders must recognize that absent-mindedness can compromise their decision-making quality. Our brains have distinct regions, such as the left frontal and parahippocampal areas, that engage in deep thinking – focused, attentive mental engagement (Wagner et al., 1998). When these brain regions are less active, the likelihood of forgetting increases. To put this insight into action, leaders should prioritize nurturing sharp focus during critical moments. By consciously directing their attention and engaging in deep thinking, leaders activate the brain regions that contribute to effective memory formation. This increased engagement strengthens memory encoding, resulting in enhanced information recall when making decisions.

Blocking

Blocking occurs when information stored in memory becomes temporarily inaccessible. Consider a situation in which you struggle to remember a word or a name. You are certain you had it in mind, but it just slipped your mind at the crucial moment of your presentation. This phenomenon is commonly known as the "tip-of-the-tongue" experience. Blocking is not selective. It affects both personal memories (episodic memory) and general world knowledge (semantic memory). Consider scenarios in which an idea or crucial piece of information is on the brink of your consciousness during a meeting but fails to emerge at the appropriate time. This can hinder effective communication and decision-making. When information is blocked, leaders can use external aids such as reference materials, digital devices, notebooks, or colleagues to retrieve the blocked information.

The first three "sins" of memory are different types of forgetting: transience, absent-mindedness, and blocking. All of them can be seen as sins of omission. When we need to recall a piece of information, it is inaccessible or unavailable. The following three "sins" are about memory distortions or inaccuracies.

Misattribution

Misattribution is when we attribute a memory or idea to an incorrect source. We may remember a piece of information but forget its origin. Misattribution of suspects in criminal cases is a notable example of misattribution, in which a face seen in one context is falsely associated with another (Belli et al., 1994). In leadership contexts, misattribution can lead to confusion and misguided decisions. For example, a manager may recall an innovative strategy and attribute it to a well-respected business leader when, in reality, the idea originated from a team member. This misattribution creates misunderstandings and leaves the team member feeling unappreciated. Leaders should exercise vigilance to prevent unintentional misattribution of credit and to ensure that recognition is directed accurately, thereby creating a sense of fairness and respect within the team. Another type of misattribution occurs when we mistakenly believe that our spontaneous thoughts or ideas are entirely original when, in reality, they originated from others, or we were simply exposed to those ideas in the past. Leaders should remain humble and open to the possibility of unintended misattributions. Even original thinkers are influenced by past experiences and external stimuli.

Suggestibility

Another memory error that goes hand in hand with misattribution is suggestibility. It occurs when memories are influenced or implanted through leading questions or comments. Misattribution contributes to the transformation of suggestions into false memories. Memory is an effortful process. Every time we recall a past event, we must exert effort to reconstruct that memory. False memories can crop up when we attempt to recall events that may not have even happened and someone suggests them to us. It occurs when we incorporate others' information into our own memories, like when we are asked misleading questions or given suggestions. In one study, participants were shown images of a car stopping at a stop sign and then asked about the car passing a yield sign. The participants often changed their memories to match the misleading question (Loftus, 1991). This is alarming, especially when considering eyewitness testimony. In another experiment, participants were shown a video of a crime and then given a set of photos to identify the perpetrator. Those who were told they were correct, even though the actual perpetrator was not in the photos, were more confident and detailed in their later recollections. In legal contexts, suggestibility has significant implications, as suggestive police interrogations have led to false confessions. Almost 70% of study participants falsely confessed to an error they did not commit (Kassin & Kiechel, 1996). Leaders in law enforcement and the legal profession should exercise caution in their interrogation techniques to avoid unjust outcomes. Our memory is not as reliable as we believe, and suggestions can sometimes lead us to remember events that never happened!

Bias

Bias occurs when our current knowledge and beliefs subconsciously distort our memories. Our memories are not static; they change over time and are influenced by our current beliefs, preconceptions, and emotions. For example, you had an opinion on a particular social issue 10 years ago. Now, your perspective may have changed, but if you try to recall what you believed back then, you will likely project your current beliefs onto your past self. You believe you were as enlightened as you are now – that is a bias in action. Another example of bias can be seen in hiring decisions. A hiring manager examines resumes for an open position and notices that one candidate graduated from a prestigious university. The hiring manager has a preconceived notion that graduates from this specific university are exceptionally competent and successful. Based on this assumption, the hiring manager may overestimate the candidate's qualifications and abilities compared to those of other candidates who may not have attended such a prestigious university but may be equally or more qualified for the position. This assumption creates a memory illusion in which the candidate's qualifications are overestimated.

Persistence

While memory often fails us in the form of forgetting things we wish to remember, such as transience, absent-mindedness, and blocking, there is another aspect of memory, known as persistence, which is the exact opposite. Persistence is about unwanted memories – information or events we cannot forget, even though we want to. Once our brains have learned to fear something, it can be difficult to erase that fear. It is most evident in people who have experienced trauma. They often cannot help but recall their traumas repeatedly despite their best efforts to suppress them. This occurs not only with traumatic events, as in post-traumatic stress disorder, but also with emotionally distressing events. Negative memories are more vividly recalled than positive ones. It seems as though the brain holds onto negative experiences more tightly. Even worse, the persistent memories often feel as vivid and intense as they did when the event first happened. This constant loop of negative thinking can prolong depressive episodes and, in extreme cases, lead to suicide. Leaders may find this aspect of memory challenging when dealing with past failures or negative feedback. The persistence of these memories can influence future decisions, causing us to be risk-averse and inhibiting our creativity. Moreover, recognizing and understanding this aspect of memory can lead to more empathetic leadership, especially when dealing with team members who may have experienced trauma or adversity.

SINS OR COSTS OF SURVIVAL?

You may wonder why our memory system is riddled with flaws. Though the seven sins of memory may initially seem like flaws, they are actually adaptive mechanisms that facilitate efficient cognitive functioning. Our memory system, as stated earlier, is not an infallible data repository. Instead, it is an adaptive mechanism that has been honed over time to increase our chances of survival. The memory system prioritizes relevance, storing essential information for survival while discarding irrelevant or obsolete details.

Consider transience as an example. It causes us to forget irrelevant information, such as where we parked at a mall last month or an old phone number. Transience serves a purpose: to clear mental space for more relevant, current information, like the key points of a business proposal or an upcoming meeting agenda. Similarly, blocking – the inability to recall certain memories due to interference, and absent-mindedness – where attention is a prerequisite for memory formation – are essential checks and balances. Without them, we would be inundated with every minutia that ever crossed our path, turning decision-making into an arduous task.

Misattribution, suggestibility, and bias, which distort memory, are byproducts of an indispensable memory feature – the capacity for generalization, crucial for learning and intelligent action. For example, our memories often lack the specifics of how we learned something, leaving us susceptible to misattributions and suggestions. However, remembering every minor detail would be taxing and, in most cases, unnecessary. False recall and recognition can also occur when we remember the gist of an experience but not its specifics. This generalization, while it can lead to distortions, is essential for learning and decision-making. Similarly, although our prior knowledge and schemas can sometimes distort our recollections, they play a crucial role in organizing our cognition and guiding memory retrieval. Persistence, the last of the seven sins of memory, is the most clearly adaptive. It is important for emotionally arousing experiences to remain in our memory, as they often indicate threats to our survival. This may sometimes result in unwanted memories, but it is a mechanism that helps us remember important information.

In this light, even the coveted "photographic memory" may not be as desirable as it seems. Imagine remembering each and every aspect of your experiences and the information you have come across. This overload may impede your ability to prioritize and filter relevant information, leading to confusion and poor decision-making. Negative experiences will persist if you are unable to forget them, impairing your judgment. In addition, constant access to a wealth of information detracts from focusing on the present, which may inhibit creative thinking.

Even though our memory system has flaws, it is intricately adapted to fulfill its purpose – not as an all-seeing photographic lens but as a cognitive tool that enables us to efficiently navigate the world and make informed decisions. Similar to the "spandrels" between structural elements in architecture, these apparent flaws are byproducts of an otherwise efficient system. As leaders, understanding these mechanisms enables us to appreciate our memory's useful yet imperfect nature. Rather than striving for a mythical "perfect" memory, we should appreciate its intriguing complexity and its many beneficial, if sometimes imperfect, mechanisms. We harness our memory's natural strengths and weaknesses to make sound, well-informed decisions, reinforcing the notion that often it is not about having more information but knowing how to use it effectively.

HOW TO REMEMBER BETTER?

How can leaders improve their memory for decision-making? Let us explore practices leaders can use to optimize the three phases of the memory system: encoding, storage, and retrieval. During the encoding phase, where information is initially processed and organized for memory storage, leaders can benefit from paying attention and visual encoding. First, paying attention is the first essential step. Whether it is remembering names at a networking event or recalling the key points from a crucial meeting, paying attention to the moment is key to making it memorable. Leaders must be fully present, immersed in the experience, and take note of the details. Since the left hemisphere of the brain is responsible for verbal encoding (Wagner et al., 1998), focusing on words and verbal communication may enhance retention. Second, leaders should also be aware that the right hemisphere of the brain plays a significant role in encoding nonverbal or visual information. Using visual aids, diagrams, or images in presentations can improve the retention of visual information.

Moving to the storage phase, leaders can benefit from the spacing effect and associative learning. Instead of cramming information into a short period, leaders can capitalize on the "spacing effect." This principle refers to the phenomenon that learning is more effective when spaced out over time as opposed to concentrated in one sitting. By spacing out learning sessions, the brain is able to consolidate information more effectively, thereby improving long-term retention. It is especially useful for absorbing complex material such as new technologies, regulations, and business strategies. In addition, associative learning is about creating associations between new information and prior knowledge or experiences. By establishing those associations, the brain is better able to access and recall the new information. Associating a newly learned leadership theory with real-world experience, for example, can make the learning process more effective and memorable.

When it comes to the retrieval phase, where stored information is accessed, leaders can create memory triggers, practice recall techniques, and maintain healthy habits. Memory triggers are stimuli that activate or enhance the recall of specific memories or experiences. The triggers can be sensory, emotional, or contextual cues that prompt us to recall past information. Consider a situation in which you are confronted with a complex strategic decision, similar to one you have experienced in the past. The familiar surroundings, conversations, or even the aroma in the air during a previous decision-making process can serve as memory triggers. These cues can help you recall how you handled the previous situation, the strategies you used, and the outcomes you achieved. This rekindling of memory not only assists in recalling relevant information but also draws parallels and applies past lessons to the current situation.

Leaders can also use recall techniques to improve memory cues during the decision-making process. For example, you can use mind mapping, a visual representation technique that allows you to map out key elements and connections related to a decision. By mapping out different components, you create a visual cue that triggers the recall of your thought process when revisiting the decision in the future. Moreover, the use of mnemonic devices, such as acronyms or rhymes, can assist in retaining complex information relevant to a decision. These techniques provide leaders with structured ways to retrieve relevant details and insights from their memory banks.

Finally, it is recommended that leaders maintain healthy habits. An essential aspect of optimizing memory triggers for decision-making lies in maintaining a healthy brain. Leaders can take a holistic approach by prioritizing factors that promote optimal brain function. Adequate sleep is a cornerstone, as it allows the brain to consolidate information acquired throughout the day. A good night's sleep improves memory retrieval, ensuring that leaders can access relevant experiences when making critical decisions. Regular physical exercise also plays a pivotal role. Physical activity increases blood flow to the brain, promoting the growth of new neurons and enhancing cognitive function. Moreover, leaders can improve their decision-making process by adhering to a balanced diet abundant in nutrients known to benefit brain health.

7

IN PEOPLE WE TRUST

Trust, as the bedrock of all social relationships, is indispensable to cooperation and social interaction. Trusting your team members means that you have a positive expectation that they will not exploit your vulnerability in uncertain situations regardless of your ability to monitor or control them. This expectation can be viewed as a form of investment in which you expose yourself to potential risks, banking on the hope that others will act in your favor or, at the very least, not harm you. Trust carries inherent risks. But why do we put ourselves in such a vulnerable position? From an energy optimization perspective, the brain constantly attempts to maintain a balance between energy consumption and an accurate interpretation of environmental inputs. When we trust someone, we do not need to engage in exhaustive cognitive processing every time we interact with them. Instead, we can rely on our established expectations of their trustworthiness, conserving cognitive resources and optimizing our brains' energy budget. Trust reduces uncertainty in interpersonal interactions. It enables us to predict their behavior, thereby reducing the uncertainty and risk involved in interacting with them. In this way, trust becomes a mental shortcut or heuristic, allowing us to navigate complex social environments without having to constantly evaluate and re-evaluate the trustworthiness of others, a process that would require substantial cognitive resources and energy. A team with a high level of trust provides a more stable environment where complex decisions can be made without constantly questioning the trustworthiness of its members.

There are two types of trust that leaders should be aware of: unconditional and conditional trust. The well-known idiom "If you fool me once, shame on you; if you fool me twice, shame on me" provides a clear distinction between the two types of trust.

UNCONDITIONAL TRUST

Unconditional trust is freely given and is not contingent on the recipient's behavior. It resembles the scenario in the idiom "If you fool me once, shame on you," in which you trust someone for the first time despite the possibility that they will betray your trust. By giving them the benefit of the doubt and believing they will act in good faith, you demonstrate unconditional trust – an innate form of trust often observed in close relationships, such as those between family members or close friends.

We often decide how trustworthy people are instantly upon meeting them, judging by their face and body language. When you decide to trust someone unconditionally, the septal area of your brain is intensely activated (Krueger et al., 2007). The septal area plays a crucial role in creating social attachment behaviors, which are the behaviors that help us form bonds with others. Recall how you felt when you met a dear friend or enjoyed a family dinner. That sense of comfort, warmth, and trust? That is our friendly septal area at work.

In addition to the septal area, the posterior cingulate cortex (PCC) plays an instrumental role in developing unconditional trust. The PCC is located roughly in the center of your brain, near the top. It plays a special role in the process known as "mentalizing." This is the process of understanding other people's thoughts and feelings, similar to attempting to predict tomorrow's weather based on today's cloud formations. The PCC uses mentalizing to understand the thoughts, feelings, and intentions of others. This ability allows your brain to assess whether a person is trustworthy. You use this mentalizing process to confirm your initial belief that your partner is trustworthy. You update your understanding of your partner's actions and intentions based on past behavior. It is like an observant gardener who, after weeks of attentive care, trusts that a particular plant will flourish given the right care. This understanding then facilitates a strong sense of mutual goodwill and social attachment.

Some people are more trusting than others. How much, if at all, is trust subject to genetic influences and thus possibly heritable? To what extent is distrust nurtured by families and immediate peers who encourage young people to be vigilant and suspicious of others? Initial empirical evidence suggests that trust is influenced by genetic factors. Some people are naturally predisposed to be more trusting, and this trait could be inherited. However, distrust is primarily shaped by socialization, often nurtured by immediate family and peers who advocate for vigilance and caution when interacting with others (Reimann et al., 2017). Understanding this distinction between trust and distrust is crucial because leaders who grew up in families that emphasized distrust may adopt a more cautious approach in professional settings.

CONDITIONAL TRUST

Unlike unconditional trust, which is trust without reservation, conditional trust depends on certain conditions or expectations. It is more calculated, strategic, and often contingent on the other party's behavior. You trust someone only if they prove they are trustworthy. A common example can be observed in people's trust in experts. This type of trust is contingent on qualifications, experience, and a track record of success. A team member named Jane who has been instructed by you to investigate a particular question of office procedure may report: "I have looked into the problem and suggest that you act in this manner." You may accept Jane's recommendation without reviewing the evidence if you trust her professional judgment. However, if Jane lacks a recognized status or is not acknowledged as an expert by her peers, it becomes more challenging for her to convince others that her recommendations are sound. When it comes to evaluating recommendations, their value is assessed not only based on their content but also on the credibility of the people making the recommendations. This is why there is typically resistance within organizations toward suggestions that come from unconventional sources or channels outside the norm.

Reciprocity is another key aspect of conditional trust. In a reciprocal relationship, one person initiates trust, giving the other person the opportunity to reciprocate. This is a common occurrence in collaborative relationships. One person initiates a reciprocal exchange by trusting the other. This initial act of trust sets the stage for a mutually beneficial exchange. This alternating pattern of trust initiation often characterizes collaboration, in which the role of the initiator can switch between the people involved. This back-and-forth of trust allows the creation of collaboration that is mutually advantageous.

Conditional trust, contingent upon expected rewards, engages the ventral tegmental area (VTA), a region associated with evaluating expected and actual rewards (Krueger et al., 2007). The VTA is located in the midbrain region of the brain. Its function is to monitor what is happening in your brain and decide when, where, and how much dopamine to release. When the VTA recognizes that something good has happened or anticipates that something good is about to happen, it releases dopamine, creating a sensation of satisfaction and reward. When you decide to trust someone conditionally, the VTA

becomes more active. It is like you are investing your trust carefully, antici-
pating the highest possible return. If the expected return is promising, the VTA
releases dopamine, producing a rewarding feeling that encourages conditional
trust. Moreover, the VTA is recruited to evaluate the expected rewards of trust
based on past interactions. If you were betrayed once and then chose to trust
the same person again without any evidence of change, and they betrayed you
again, the fault would lie with you for not learning from your past experience
("Fool me twice, shame on me."). The next time you carefully consider
whether to trust your partner based on past experiences, your decision-making
process may take longer. It takes time to cultivate trust, as others gradually
earn your trust through benevolence, competence, honesty, openness, and
reliability. These five dimensions of trust collectively aim to reduce uncertainty, ultimately enabling you to bestow your trust on them.

OXYTOCIN: THE TRUST HORMONE

Let us add oxytocin to the mental process of trust. Oxytocin is a hormone
produced in the hypothalamus, an almond-sized structure located near the
base of your brain. Once produced, oxytocin is transported to the pituitary
gland, where it is stored and released as needed into the bloodstream. In one
study, after an intranasal application before the participants made their
decisions, participants with higher oxytocin levels were more willing to take
financial risks, entrusting more money to their counterparts than those who
received a placebo (Kosfeld et al., 2005). Remarkably, this increase in trust
occurred even though their expectations for investment returns remained
constant. However, it was not a blanket increase in all forms of risk-taking. In
experiments without human interaction, the oxytocin-boosted participants
behaved no differently than the placebo group. The key is that oxytocin did
not make all participants more generous or risky. It only influenced their
trusting behavior in a social context, suggesting that our biology functions
differently in social versus nonsocial contexts.

When you are interacting with someone you trust, oxytocin sends signals to
your brain that the connection is safe and supportive. This "backstage pass"
allows you to lower your guard and form a deeper bond with this person. In
fact, oxytocin comes into play even when you interact with dogs. The gaze of a
dog induces a surge of oxytocin, which increases your trust in them. Simultaneously, your brain also receives rewarding "feel-good" signals from
dopamine, especially if the interaction is positive or beneficial. For example,

you delegate a task to Joe, who completes it as you expected. This positive outcome of your trust in Joe triggers dopamine release as your brain registers this as a rewarding interaction (you trusted Joe, and he did not disappoint). The consistent, reliable behavior of Joe triggers oxytocin release, which reinforces the trust and bonding between you two. In essence, oxytocin and dopamine are like a dynamic duo in a band. Oxytocin sets the stage for trust and bonding, and dopamine hits the right notes to make the interaction pleasurable and worth repeating. Together, they play a pivotal role in how we form and maintain trusting relationships.

NEGATIVE SIDE OF TRUST

Not all effects of oxytocin are positive. First, oxytocin's ability to increase trust can be a double-edged sword. Oxytocin can make us more trusting, even toward those we know to be untrustworthy. This increased trust makes us more susceptible to betrayal. The implications for leaders are profound. Sometimes, a tendency to trust can result in poor judgment or allow dishonest people to exploit a situation. Although trust is typically a positive trait of leaders, an overreliance on it, possibly fueled by oxytocin, may lead to adverse outcomes.

Another intriguing aspect of oxytocin's effect is its ability to reduce cooperation with those outside our social groups, resulting in parochial trust. We tend to place more trust in people who share our social identity – those who are one of us (De Dreu et al., 2010, 2011). The shared identity makes decision-makers more empathetic and willing to take others' perspectives. By contrast, when people do not share our social identity, we are more likely to cast doubt on out-group members' intentions. Leaders need to be aware that trust can lead to preferential treatment of in-group members. By recognizing this potential pitfall, leaders can ensure a more balanced approach in which trust is cultivated but tempered with inclusion and fairness.

8

WHEN MY FACE MEETS YOUR EYES

Think about your most recent team meeting. You, as a leader, were not only speaking to your team members, but you were also "reading" them – how they felt, whether they agreed or disagreed, whether they understood your points, or whether they had something to say. This process of "reading" primarily happens through faces. Faces are the most expressive parts of our bodies, uniquely designed to convey a wide range of human emotions, from the subtle flicker of doubt to the broad grin of agreement. Whether it is furrowed brows of confusion, intense gazes of concentration, or raised eyebrows of surprise, each facial cue tells a story. But this is not a one-way street. In fact, it is likely your team members pay even more attention to your face. Your facial expressions as a leader guide the team members' interpretations of your intentions and expectations. A stern face may signal determination. A relaxed face may suggest openness. All of these cues from faces subconsciously shape your responses, guide your interactions, and influence your decisions (Atkinson & Adolphs, 2011). In this chapter, we will explore why our brains prioritize facial information and how this innate focus on faces influences our interactions and decisions. We will also take a close look at how our brain's adept handling of facial information can either support or hinder our decision-making.

THE "FACE EFFECT" IN THE HUMAN BRAIN

Faces captivate our attention more than any other object. When viewing scenes containing faces, our eyes predominantly fixate on them, taking just over one-tenth of a second to do so. There is no other object that captures our attention so rapidly. The rapid attraction to faces, also known as the "face effect," is involuntary. It forms first impressions, assigns preferences, and discerns emotional states and personality traits (Kanwisher & Yovel, 2006).

The ability to recognize faces is not something we consciously acquire. Instead, it is rooted in our biology and develops naturally as we mature and interact with our environment. Faces are treated differently than other objects, suggesting the existence of specialized mechanisms distinct from general object recognition systems. These mechanisms have evolved because of the important social role that face perception plays in human survival and communication. As a result, our brains have become particularly adept at processing facial information, which reflects the significance of faces for social perception and interaction. This inherent aptitude is so powerful that we sometimes even see faces in inanimate objects – think about the last time you spotted a "face" in the patterns of clouds, a carpet, or a pancake (Palmer & Clifford, 2020).

An essential element in our ability to recognize and interpret faces is a brain region called the fusiform face area (FFA). The word "fusiform" derives from the Latin word "fusus," meaning "shape" or "form." In the term FFA, "fusiform" is used to describe the brain region's fusiform shape. This region is highly activated when we view faces, indicating its importance in facial perception. As the name suggests, the FFA's primary role is facial perception, integrating visual cues, attention, memory, and emotions to create a unified understanding of faces. The FFA becomes highly activated when we view faces. More importantly, it responds only to human faces, not objects such as furniture or trees (Kanwisher & Yovel, 2006).

The FFA does not operate in isolation. It interacts with the superior temporal sulcus (STS), a trench-like structure crucial for social competence situated on the outer side of the temporal lobe that is essential for social competence. The STS resides in the temporal lobe, a brain region responsible for memory, language, and sensory processing. The partnership between the FFA and STS enables us to perceive and interpret facial expressions in order to guide our social responses, such as approaching, sharing, fleeing, or defending. It also plays a role in tracking the direction of others' gazes and evaluating trustworthiness from facial images.

The FFA also collaborates with the occipital facial area (OFA) and the amygdala, which assign both individual and gender identities based on the configuration of the facial features and process emotional content. Specifically, certain cells in the amygdala, known as "face cells," become active when our eyes fixate on a human face, stimulating memory-forming activity in the hippocampus, which is responsible for information processing and memory formation. The face cells' firing speed correlates with memory retention; faster firing results in a better memory of the face observed. Familiar faces cause slower firing, indicating that they are already stored in memory (Staudigl et al., 2022). Our brain's ability to encode and store facial representations is, therefore, influenced by our past experiences. We are exposed to a vast number of faces throughout our lives, and this exposure helps develop specialized neural circuitry for face processing. Experience with faces, including those of family and friends, shapes the brain's ability to recognize and remember specific people. Maternity-ward nurses who are regularly exposed to newborn faces are adept at distinguishing infants by their faces (Cassia et al., 2009).

WHEN YOU SEE MY FACE

What happens when my face meets your eyes? Let us take a detailed look at how our brains process faces. When light reflected from a face enters our eyes, the retina absorbs it and sends it along the optic nerve to the lateral geniculate nucleus (LGN), a relay center in the thalamus. This region is essential for transmitting sensory information to the cerebral cortex, our brain's main control center, and initiating facial recognition.

Within 16 milliseconds (for reference, a second has 1,000 milliseconds), our brains begin to categorize faces as either in-group (those who look like us) or out-group (those who look different from us). This time frame is so fleeting that we are unaware that we have seen the face. However, this reflexive processing has a substantial impact on team dynamics and decision-making. For example, a brief exposure to an aggressive face can subliminally prime negative stereotypes and increase aggression toward out-groups.

Within 40 milliseconds, the brain's LGN activates the process of creating a visual representation for the cortex, merging data from both eyes. Simultaneously, the brain interprets nonverbal social cues, such as eye contact, which may signify confidence or a desire for connection (Rule et al., 2012). By contrast, avoiding eye contact may hint at discomfort or disinterest. As our brain processes those cues, it is making split-second judgments about social hierarchy, guiding us to navigate complex social interactions.

Around 50 milliseconds, the visual cortex begins registering finer details like the face shape, eye color, or hairstyle. At this point, you have probably already formed your judgment about whether someone is extraverted or not. Those judgments are often accurate (Borkenau et al., 2009).

By 70 milliseconds, brain regions mentioned in the previous section, such as FFA, OFA, and STS, tell you that you are looking at a face and start to categorize its gender and age. At 90 milliseconds, those brain regions allow you to recognize that the face belongs to a specific person, prompting your brain to compare it with previously seen faces.

Within 100 milliseconds, the brain processes racial cues, forming initial judgments about a stranger's likability, trustworthiness, competence, and aggressiveness. It takes as little as one-tenth of a second to judge the competence of candidates in gubernatorial elections, based solely on the candidates' facial appearance and without prior knowledge about the candidates. Exposure to the face for 100 milliseconds is sufficient to judge people's traits. Remarkably, people's competence judgments collected before the elections in 2006 predicted 68.6% of the 89 gubernatorial races and 72.4% of the Senate races (Todorov et al., 2005). Intriguingly, giving the brain more time does not necessarily improve judgment accuracy but rather bolsters confidence in the initial judgments. When asked to deliberate, participants were effectively adding unnecessary noise to their judgments, diminishing their accuracy (Ballew & Todorov, 2007). More time does not necessarily improve accuracy in your decision-making. We often fail to anticipate how little information we use when making decisions (Hall et al., 2007; Todorov et al., 2009).

By 130 milliseconds, additional cues like clothing are considered. People consistently associate competence with expensive clothing, regardless of the time they are given to form their impression, even after they are offered financial incentives not to do so and even after they are provided with information about their profession and income (Oh et al., 2019). Since people judge others' competence instantaneously, one suggestion for making high-quality decisions is not to expose decision-makers to such noisy information to prevent erroneous judgments.

All those judgments occur subconsciously before you are even aware of them. The difference between the speed of subconscious processing (around 100 milliseconds) and conscious awareness (approximately 300–500 milliseconds) is due to the distinct nature of brain processing mechanisms. The subconscious brain can process information rapidly and parallelly, while conscious thought is more sequential, requiring more time. Our brains, it seems, are perfectly attuned to form instinctive, snap judgments about faces. As a leader, understanding this automatic tendency can help you be mindful of its potential impact on your decision-making.

HOW FACES EXPRESS EMOTIONS

One reason our brains are naturally drawn to faces is because they are incredibly expressive and broadcast our emotional states, intentions, and reactions. Facial expressions – whether it is a smile with closed lips, a twitching nose, tearful eyes, a flushed face, or clenched jaws – are fleeting emotional signals that carry important information about our social partners. The human face is an exquisite communication organ capable of conveying an expansive array of emotions, some of which are highly subtle (Cowen & Keltner, 2020). For example, a slightly followed brow with eyes slightly narrowed denotes puzzlement; that same expression, when accompanied by a slightly down-turned mouth, displays skepticism; the slightly upturned corners of a mouth with parted lips signal happiness or amusement; while tightly closed lips can signify distrust. When leaders are attuned to others' emotions, the brain maximizes energy efficiency to navigate the social environment, enabling more effective communication at work.

Human facial expressivity is particularly evident when two people converse directly, literally "face to face." In face-to-face conversations, human facial expressions underscore spoken words, reinforcing or undermining the meaning conveyed through spoken statements. A vibrant play of expressions creates a shadow dialogue behind the verbal exchange, providing an emotional subtext often as vital as the spoken words themselves. This extensive use of facial communication is also subject to manipulation. Negotiators and poker players may deliberately control their expressions to mislead others. Moreover, the visual layer of information transmitted through facial expressions is notably absent in written communications like emails or letters. It helps explain why written communications so often lead to misunderstandings. They are missing facially expressive content. Adding a smile "emoticon" to an email is an attempt to express a positive feeling that one suspects is not conveyed by the words alone (Wilkins, 2017). In our current world, which is increasingly reliant on digital communication, face-to-face interaction is still irreplaceable.

FACES AS SOCIAL CUES

The human face is also a rich source of social information that can shape our decisions and behaviors. Our brains effortlessly extract social information, providing insights into someone's identities, including gender, ethnicity, age, and cultural affiliations. Such information is important for social bonding, cooperation, and the complex navigation of social dynamics. Although faces naturally capture human attention, human brains do not respond to all human faces in the same way.

Generally, we are better at recognizing faces of our own race than faces of other races (Golby et al., 2001). This phenomenon is known as the other-race effect. Our brain's FFA shows more significant activation when responding to same-race faces. This greater activation is linked to memory, attention, and emotion, leading to a superior memory for same-race faces. Moreover, parts of the medial temporal lobe, like the left fusiform cortex and the right para-hippocampal and hippocampal areas, also show different levels of activation, correlating with memory performance.

The other-race effect is not confined to the United States but is seen glob-ally. It begins early in life and intensifies over time (Sangrigoli & De Schonen, 2004). The first thing a newborn infant sees within a minute or so is a face. It is the mother's face, and the baby sees it just after being placed in her arms (Jessen & Grossmann, 2016). As children enter adolescence, the race-selective response only becomes stronger, which suggests that life experiences may be a contributing factor. Our brain builds a preference for the faces we see every day and over time, at the expense of skills needed to recognize others less relevant. The other-race effect can be considered a sign that our perceptive powers are shaped by what we see. When we do not have sufficient exposure to faces from other races, we feel, "They all look alike." With sufficient exposure, the other-race effect can be reduced. Children who are adopted by parents of a different race do not exhibit the classic other-race effect. For example, Chinese and Vietnamese children who had been adopted by white families were equally good at recognizing white and Asian faces (Telzer et al., 2013).

Our brains' preferential response to same-race faces extends to many decisions, including leadership selection. Although we may believe that the criteria for choosing a leader are qualities like competence, intelligence, honesty, and trustworthiness, our judgments are often influenced by rapid, automatic assessments of a candidate's facial appearance. Chief executive officers in Fortune 1,000 companies are likely to have faces that are judged to be competent and mature (Rule & Ambady, 2008). In politics, candidates with faces judged to be competent are more likely to be elected to political office (Ballew & Todorov, 2007). Moreover, people tend to vote for candidates who are facially similar to themselves. This tendency is even stronger when they are independent voters and do not support a particular political party (Bailenson et al., 2008). The other-race effect also provides a lens for understanding stereotypes and prejudices. Faces function as identity tags in social interactions, and a misperception can lead to unintentional stereotyping. For leaders striving to create an inclusive environment, acknowledging and addressing this innate tendency can be helpful to connect more effectively with their audiences and challenge their biases.

One particular facial trait that is associated with leadership selection is called the facial width-to-height ratio (fWHR). It is a ratio of the distance between the left and right zygion, which are the most lateral points on the cheekbones, by the distance between the midbrow and the highest point on the upper lip (Wong et al., 2011). Men with a higher fWHR are more likely to be perceived as dominant and assertive, and thus more likely to be selected as leaders. CEOs of leading UK companies have been found to have greater fWHRs and were perceived as having higher dominance or success (Alrajih & Ward, 2014). One explanation is that men with a higher fWHR tend to have higher levels of testosterone, which may contribute to their dominant and assertive behavior (Carré et al., 2009), as well as aggression and status-striving (Lefevre et al., 2013). It has been found that men with higher fWHR were more likely to exploit others' trust and were more willing to cheat in order to increase their financial gain (Costa et al., 2017; Haselhuhn & Wong, 2011). Firms led by CEOs perceived to be more trustworthy, which was associated with lower fWHR, attracted more negative media attention in the wake of corporate scandals (Heyden et al., 2022). Additionally, neuroimaging studies have shown that people with higher fWHR have larger amygdalae, a brain region involved in processing emotions and social information, which may play a role in their ability to accurately perceive and respond to social cues. Recognizing how facial features can unconsciously impact decisions about trust, leadership selection, and public perceptions is critical for leaders aiming to make more informed and unbiased decisions. The ongoing research in this field continues to unravel the complex relationships between facial characteristics, genetics, personality, and leadership potential, shedding light on new dimensions of human psychology and social interactions in leadership roles.

9

PERSONALITY DRIVES LEADERS' DECISION-MAKING

How do you describe your personality? Courageous? Stubborn? Confident? Extroverted? Flamboyant and volatile? Steady and reserved? What is personality, exactly? Where does your personality come from? How do personality traits influence leaders' decision-making? This chapter focuses on those inquiries.

WHAT IS PERSONALITY?

Personality is a pattern of human behavior. Personality is expressed through a pattern of behavior over time and functions as a predictor of a person's decisions. There are three personality features that most scientists have agreed upon. First, personality is stable. Although some people's personality traits are more malleable than others', personality does not change from moment to moment, unlike emotions, thoughts, and behaviors. As a result, knowing someone's personality allows us to predict their decisions. Second, personalities are individually different. It is part of the explanation for why each person behaves somewhat differently in a given context, and we can use personality as a guide to identify distinct personality types among groups of people (Gerlach et al., 2018). Third, personality is multicomponent. The way to organize and arrange enduring characteristics, behaviors, motives, thoughts, and emotions is called personality structure. For example, one prominent model of personality structure is the five-factor model, also known as the Big Five. This model posits that personality can be characterized across five broad dimensions: openness to experience, conscientiousness, extraversion, agreeableness, and neuroticism. These traits are often seen as emotional–motivational dispositional traits triggered by particular stimuli. We will discuss it in more detail shortly.

WHERE DOES PERSONALITY COME FROM?

One interdisciplinary view, drawn from psychology, neuroscience, and physiology, holds that our personality resides in our brain (Dubois et al., 2020). Personality is an outcome of the interaction between genetics and environment. Put differently, personality is the result of nature and nurture.

Nature

Nature refers to a person's genotype – the specific set of genes inherited from one's parents. Half of our genes are inherited from our biological father, and the remaining half are inherited from our biological mother. Genes are the fundamental units of heredity as they contain the information that parents pass down to their children. Genes combine in unique ways to create the genetic makeup that makes you unique. Genes serve as the instruction manual for the production of particular proteins, which are indispensable tools in our cells. The proteins then perform a variety of functions within the body, from building physical structures like hair and skin to producing neurotransmitters such as oxytocin, dopamine, and serotonin that regulate brain function and behavior. Similarly, the neurotransmitter dopamine, which plays a crucial role in the brain's reward system, is also influenced by genetic variation. A decrease in dopamine levels has been linked to increased risk-taking behavior (Ryding et al., 2021). Moreover, gene variants can contribute to differences in serotonin levels among individuals, with lower levels potentially indicating a predisposition to depression or overeating and higher levels often linked to feelings of well-being and happiness. Therefore, genotypes can influence the structure and function of the brain, which, in turn, impacts behavior (DeYoung et al., 2010).

Genetic influences on personality have been found to extend to leadership traits. Researchers have demonstrated a genetic basis for personality traits. A study of about 807 pairs of twins, including 490 identical twins (who share nearly identical genetic material) and 317 fraternal twins (who share on average about 50% of their genetic material), found that genetics played a big role in the Big Five personality traits, with about 50% of the differences between people being due to genetics (Loehlin et al., 1998).

How much do genetic factors influence the ability to hold a leadership position? The estimated heritability is about 30%. This indicates that approximately 30% of the individual differences in leadership role occupancy can be attributed to genetic factors, whereas the remaining 70% is influenced by nonshared environmental factors. Some of the genetic factors that influence leadership are similar to those influencing personality variables (Arvey et al., 2006). While genetic factors accounted for a substantial portion of the variance in leadership, the findings highlighted the importance of environmental factors in leadership.

Interaction of Genetics and Environment

Our brains are also changed by environmental factors we are exposed to throughout our lives. Environmental factors range from cells, nutrients, leadership training, mentoring to cultural exposure. A person with a genetic predisposition toward extraversion may not develop an extroverted personality if they grow up in an environment that discourages social interaction. Similarly, people with leadership potential may have parents who create an environment that nurtures leadership traits. At a young age, they may be recognized and given special opportunities to learn about leadership both in school and at work (Arvey et al., 2007). Moreover, people who are not genetically predisposed to engage in leadership behaviors can still develop leadership skills through exposure to environmental factors such as leadership training. Just because we have a certain set of genes does not necessarily mean that they will manifest in our appearance or behavior. The expression of genes, or which ones are turned "on" or "off," is influenced by many environmental factors. The process of genes being turned "on" or "off" is called gene regulation, which is influenced by environmental factors such as diet, exercise, aging, formative years, significant life events, and chronic stress from work. Gene expression can differ between genetically identical individuals, such as identical twins. As a result, even though identical twins share the same genetic material, they can still display variations in some characteristics due to individual-specific environmental experiences, such as personal hobbies and interests, educational experiences, friendships and social interactions, personal goals and aspirations, exposure to different cultures and environments, and life events that are unique to each individual (Loehlin et al., 1998).

Our brain structure is not only determined by genetics but also adapts and changes in response to our life experiences. Neural plasticity, the ability of the nervous system to change, is important in understanding how environmental and social factors affect brain development and function over time (Oakes, 2017). Critical periods are times when specific neural connections must be made for proper neural development, which can explain the "use it or lose it" nature of some abilities. Poverty has been associated with changes in brain activity during infancy, particularly in critical periods (Parameshwaran et al., 2021). Children from low-income families experience slower neural growth due to a lack of environmental stimuli or increased exposure to daily stressors, such as family conflict. A lack of access to education and healthy diets also affects cognitive development. Trauma can cause epigenetic changes in brain cells, mostly likely due to elevated stress hormone levels.

It is particularly important to recognize that genetics play a *necessary* but *insufficient* role in our personality traits. It is the *gene-environment interaction* that determines our traits (Turkheimer, 2000). For genes to be expressed, it entails environmental stimuli (e.g., nutrients, upbringing, leaders' past experience, and leadership training). Collectively, they shape our personality traits and behavior.

THE BIG FIVE

The Big Five, also known as the five-factor model of personality, stands out as the most extensively researched personality model linked to leadership (Judge et al., 2002). This model comprises five key dimensions: extraversion, conscientiousness, openness, agreeableness, and neuroticism.

Extraversion

Extraversion has the strongest positive correlation with leadership. Extroverts are more involved in social activities and are superior at decoding social information than introverts (Li et al., 2010). They have reduced activity in response to stimuli in some brain regions, including the thalamus, anterior cingulate cortex, and dorsolateral prefrontal cortex, which keep the brain aroused. As a result, they need more environmental stimuli to remain energized. This explains why people with high levels of extraversion are more inclined to take risks and seek out novel experiences, which can influence their decision-making process. Extraversion is correlated with the volume of the medial orbitofrontal cortex, a brain region involved in processing reward information (De Young et al., 2010). Extraversion is an emotional trait related to the elicitation of positive affect, desire, and incentive-reward motivation by signals of reward. In simpler terms, this trait involves how emotional experiences are triggered and how they motivate us to seek out rewarding stimuli. This trait can be viewed as a measure of an individual's sensitivity to rewarding incentives (Depue & Collins, 1999). Of the five personality factors, extraversion was the best predictor of leader emergence (Reichard et al., 2011).

Conscientiousness

Conscientiousness is another personality trait associated with leadership (Strang & Kuhnert, 2009). It refers to a person's propensity to be organized, diligent, and reliable in their behavior. Conscientious people are careful, thorough, and attentive to details and have a strong sense of responsibility and self-discipline. This personality trait plays a significant role in influencing leaders' decision-making processes. Research has shown that people high in conscientiousness tend to have a larger prefrontal cortex, a brain region associated with executive functions such as planning, impulse control, and decision-making. This anatomical difference provides them with enhanced cognitive control, allowing them to evaluate options more thoroughly and consider the long-term consequences of their decisions (DeYoung et al., 2010). Conscientious people also show stronger connections between the prefrontal cortex and the amygdala. This connection enables them to regulate emotional responses to risks or uncertainties, ensuring that decisions are grounded in rational analysis rather than impulsive reactions. Moreover, people with a high level of conscientiousness exhibit elevated dopamine activity in response to achieving goals and meeting expectations. This heightened responsiveness drives them to make decisions that align with their long-term goals and the organization's success. Recent research demonstrates that companies with more conscientious CEOs exhibit greater strategic rigidity and are less likely to allocate funds to areas with uncertain returns or engage in strategic change. However, when conscientious CEOs do pursue such initiatives, they do so with a more calculated approach, which reduces the perception of risk.

Openness

Openness refers to the degree to which a person is open to new experiences, ideas, and perspectives. People with high levels of openness are typically imaginative, inquisitive, and willing to explore unconventional ideas. They often have a wide range of interests and a penchant for creativity. People with high levels of openness exhibit distinct brain activity patterns compared to those with lower levels of openness. One prominent feature of openness is the connectivity between the neocortex and the default mode network (DNM). The DMN is a network of brain regions that are active when we are not focused on the outside world and the mind is at rest. It is associated with self-referential thinking, daydreaming, and introspection. People with high levels of openness demonstrate enhanced connectivity within the DMN, facilitating the generation of diverse ideas and perspectives. This heightened connectivity enables leaders to consider unconventional solutions and innovative strategies when faced with complex decisions. Moreover, the anterior cingulate cortex, a brain region involved in detecting conflicts and monitoring cognitive control, has been found to be more active in individuals with high openness. This heightened activity allows open-minded people to detect discrepancies between diverse ideas or perspectives, creating a deeper understanding of potential trade-offs and facilitating more nuanced decision-making processes.

In addition, the neurotransmitter dopamine plays a pivotal role in understanding the influence of openness on decision-making processes. Dopamine is associated with reward processing and motivation. Openness is linked to variations in dopamine receptor genes, which modulate dopamine-related neural pathways. This finding suggests that people with a high level of openness may be more motivated by the intrinsic reward of exploring new possibilities and taking risks, thereby influencing their willingness to make bold decisions that can lead to novel outcomes.

Openness is linked to cognitive flexibility – the ability to switch between different cognitive tasks or mental sets. This cognitive flexibility is supported by interactions between the prefrontal cortex and other brain regions. Open-minded individuals tend to have more adaptable neural networks, allowing them to switch between various modes of thinking and problem-solving. A recent study analyzing data from over 1,300 studies and a staggering two million participants found a direct link between cognitive abilities and activity levels. Open-minded people have a distinct advantage when it comes to cognitive skills like acquiring knowledge and remembering information (Stanek & Ones, 2023). Open-mindedness goes hand in hand with enhanced cognitive performance.

Agreeableness

Agreeableness refers to an individual's inclination to be cooperative, considerate, and compassionate in social interactions. People with a high level of agreeableness prioritize empathy and the well-being of others. High agreeableness is associated with distinct patterns of brain activity related to social cognition and empathy. Leaders with a high level of agreeableness are typically more attuned to the emotional states of their team members and stakeholders, as well as more receptive to feedback and divergent viewpoints. This cognitive trait is associated with the activity of the anterior cingulate cortex, a brain region linked to conflict monitoring and emotional regulation. Moreover, agreeableness has implications for how leaders handle conflicts and negotiations. Leaders with a high level of agreeableness may prioritize maintaining positive relationships and avoiding conflict. This preference may influence their decision-making style to lean toward compromise and finding win-win solutions. This can be advantageous for promoting team cohesion and sustaining a collaborative work environment.

Neuroticism

Neuroticism is a person's propensity to experience negative emotions such as anxiety, worry, and mood instability. Neurotic people are more likely to react strongly to stressors and display emotional volatility. Neuroticism is associated with increased activation of the amygdala, a brain region crucial for processing emotions, especially fear and threat-related emotions. Highly neurotic individuals have stronger amygdala responses to emotionally charged stimuli, which influences their decision-making by causing them to focus more on negative information and exhibit a bias toward threat-related cues. This personality trait can lead to overly pessimistic evaluations of situations and outcomes, which may influence leaders to err on the side of caution or even indecision (Bacanli, 2006; Brooks, 2011). Moreover, neurotic people often show decreased prefrontal cortex activity during emotionally charged tasks, suggesting decreased cognitive control in such situations. This diminished cognitive control can lead to impulsive decisions driven by heightened negative emotions. Furthermore, the stress response system, including the hypothalamic-pituitary-adrenal (HPA) axis, is strongly associated with neuroticism. In stressful situations, neurotic individuals may have a more sensitive stress response, leading to elevated cortisol levels. This heightened stress response can impact decision-making by impairing cognitive functioning and reducing the ability to think rationally under pressure.

In terms of leadership, the influence of neuroticism on decision-making can have both positive and negative implications. On the one hand, leaders high in neuroticism may be more attuned to potential risks and threats, resulting in cautious decision-making that minimizes potential negative outcomes. On the other hand, excessive neuroticism can lead to decision paralysis, avoidance of necessary risks, and difficulty adapting to changing circumstances.

DARK TRIAD

The dark triad personality traits refer to three co-occurring socially aversive yet nonpathological personality traits: narcissism, psychopathy, and Machiavellianism (Paulhus & Williams, 2002; Wang, 2019). It is crucial to prevent the wrong people from gaining power. People with dark triad traits are more likely to pursue and attain positions of power, as they are often skilled at manipulating and exploiting others. This can make them particularly adept at ascending to positions of power, as they may be more risk-taking and competitive. They may be more likely to use manipulation or other unethical tactics to achieve their goals, without regard for the harm they cause to others in the process.

Psychopathy

Psychopathy is a trait characterized by a lack of empathy or remorse, impulsivity, and a tendency toward antisocial behavior. About 1% of the population may exhibit psychopathic behavior, whereas among senior executives, psychopaths are between four and a hundred times more prevalent in positions of power than the general population (Babiak et al., 2010). One reason is that psychopaths are attracted to the pace and volatility of today's hypercompetitive workplaces (Boddy, 2015). The psychopathic trait is associated with decreased activity in the ventromedial prefrontal cortex (vmPFC) and amygdala. The decreased activation in the vmPFC explains why psychopaths are incapable of empathizing with others and are "blind" to the fear expressed by others (Decety et al., 2013). Moreover, the decreased activation in the amygdala explains the psychopaths' decreased response to fear-inducing stimuli (Blair, 2010). It is thus the psychopaths' deficiency in empathizing with others and recognizing others' fear that prompts them to callously exploit others with emotional detachment.

Narcissism

Narcissism is characterized by an inflated sense of self-importance, entitlement, and a need for admiration. Narcissists are hypersensitive to what other people think of them, engage in excessive self-promotion, seek constant validation, and tend to exploit interpersonal relationships for personal gain (Den Hartog et al., 2018). They exhibit distinct patterns of brain activity related to self-perception and reward processing. The brain's reward system, which includes regions like the nucleus accumbens, is activated more strongly in response to self-relevant stimuli in individuals with high narcissism. This heightened response to self-referential cues contributes to their pursuit of attention and admiration, as such stimuli activate the brain's pleasure centers. In addition, the anterior insula, a brain region involved in processing emotions such as empathy, is less active in narcissists. This reduced activity is associated with a diminished ability to recognize others' emotional states and empathize with them. A lack of empathy can influence decision-making by causing narcissistic leaders to prioritize their own goals and desires over the well-being of their team or organization.

Narcissistic leaders typically exhibit overconfidence and a bias toward positive self-evaluation. This cognitive bias can influence their decision-making by leading them to overlook potential risks or underestimate challenges. Additionally, the dorsomedial prefrontal cortex, a region associated with self-reflection and self-awareness, is less active in narcissists. This diminished self-awareness can impair their ability to critically evaluate their own decisions and behaviors, potentially leading to risk-seeking and ego-driven decisions (Buyl et al., 2017). Narcissistic leaders engineer a bold vision to motivate followers (Galvin et al., 2010). In contrast to the bold, socialized vision articulated by charismatic leaders, narcissistic leaders' vision focuses more on the leaders' personal gain than the interests of their followers and organization. As a result, narcissists are prone to rise in organizational rank (Prundeanu et al., 2021), which may be counterproductive for firms (Ham et al., 2018).

Machiavellianism

Machiavellianism is a strategic and manipulative approach to interpersonal relationships, often with an emphasis on gaining personal gain. Machiavellians are strategic thinkers. They know all the right things to say in front of people. Machiavellianism, manifested by the social behaviors of manipulating others for personal, self-serving goals, is undergirded by the trade-off between two psychological processes of empathy: emotional contagion and mentalizing (Bagozzi et al., 2013). In comparison to those with low Machiavellian traits, those with high Machiavellian traits exhibit greater emotional sharing with others (i.e., emotional contagion) but a lower capability for mentalizing. They achieve their popularity and maintain their power through coercive strategies while mitigating the fallout of their coercive behavior through carefully calibrated acts of kindness. When necessary, they can be aggressive and then quickly "make nice" to calm any ruffled feathers. They are both loved *and* feared by others. Their well-adjusted social and emotional skills, coupled with a moderate propensity for social dominance and rule-breaking, may be advantageous or disadvantageous, depending on the environment (Hartl et al., 2020).

IMPACT ON LEADER SELECTION

Personality traits provide elaborate explanations for why some leaders are almost always more cautious or impetuous (e.g., McMullen et al., 2009), why some vigilantly show great attention to detail while others focus on the big picture (e.g., Förster & Higgins, 2005), and why some are patient while others behave somewhat recklessly (e.g., Hamstra et al., 2011) in pursuing their goals. As you can see, people with dark triad traits gravitate toward positions of power and influence. They enjoy exerting power and control over others. They are adept at navigating organizational environments and thrive in such environments. As we come to understand the harm they can cause, dark triad traits are the ones we should stay away from. Two recommendations have been proposed to mitigate their destructive impact: do not hire people with dark triad traits, and if they are already in your organization, do not promote them.

10

INTUITIVE DECISION-MAKING AND GUT FEELING

When it comes to deciding whether to hire a job candidate, you can approach it in different ways. One approach is to create criteria that include requirements and preferences, where we consider all relevant factors, rate each factor, and then calculate a score. This analytical approach is known as a deliberative strategy. By contrast, an intuitive approach to making this decision is to simply ask yourself, "Can I work with this person?" and follow your gut feeling. A prevailing view in leadership literature is that leaders' decisions should be rational, analytical, strategic, data-driven, and evidence-informed. Intuition, on the other hand, is often regarded with skepticism and doubt. It is commonly seen as mysterious and unexplainable, or, at worst, as something unreliable. Our culture is filled with sayings like "look before you leap" and "think before you act," which imply that our instincts are often flawed.

However, intuition can sometimes be just as good or even better than decisions made through deliberative thinking. It is biologically impossible for us to make every single decision by collecting all available information, conducting a cost-benefit analysis, deliberating on pros and cons, and finally reaching a decision. As mentioned in Chapter 1, our brain is a very energy-expensive organ. If we make a decision about what pen we should use to take meeting notes in the same way we allocate resources for an organization's growth in the next five years, our brain will soon run out of fuel. To optimize energy use, our brain often makes decisions by using our intuition or gut feeling.

WHAT IS INTUITIVE DECISION-MAKING?

Intuitive decision-making is defined as "affectively charged judgments that arise through rapid, nonconscious, and holistic associations" (Dane & Pratt, 2007, p. 40). The definition has two key points. First, intuitions are thought to be "affectively charged." Intuitions have an emotional component, often reflected by the term "gut *feeling*." This is supported by research indicating that intuitive decisions are connected to the neurophysiological systems linked to emotion (Lieberman, 2000). In Chapter 3, we learned that human emotions are aroused faster than the cognitive system in the brain. We feel *before* we think. The emotion-laden, gut feeling decision-making process is fast and subconscious, enabling us to make decisions without an extensive search for information, evidence, or data. Lying, for example, is probably more often the result of panic than of elaborate Machiavellian scheming. When confronted with a challenging situation, our brain's stress response can trigger a heightened state of anxiety. In such moments of heightened stress, the prospect of mitigating the distress becomes a priority. Dishonesty, like lying, can appear as a means to achieve this relief. By providing false information, people may hope to escape negative consequences or appease the emotional turmoil they are experiencing. In a way, dishonesty offers a short-term solution to managing the distressing emotions brought on by stressful situations (Tabatabaeian et al., 2015). In most cases, resorting to dishonesty as a coping mechanism is not a conscious choice.

Another key point in the definition of intuition is that intuitive decisions are made based on a subconscious assessment of the available information. Our intuitions come from our past knowledge and experiences that are stored and processed in the brain. They represent a form of immediate understanding or cognition without conscious reasoning or thought processes. Our brain rapidly compares new information with stored memories and experiences, resulting in an intuitive response. This is why intuition is formed faster than the blink of an eye and why we often struggle to provide a detailed account of our intuitive judgment. Sometimes, we may not even recognize the specific aspects of the problem to which we are responding. Intuition relies on intricate, rapid brain processing that transpires beneath the threshold of conscious awareness. "Humans are hybrid decision-makers with unique approaches to moral choices, honed over time and altered by their own distinctive experiences" (Wallach & Allen, 2009, p. 178). Neither our day-to-day nor our moral judgments are linear thought processes.

It is easy for us to accept the idea that our bodies are governed by automatic systems, allowing us to carry out essential functions like digestion and respiration without conscious effort. However, when it comes to our thoughts and actions, we often resist the idea that they are predetermined and unconscious. Yet, experimental evidence indicates that actions occur before our brain becomes consciously aware of them. Our brain's interpretive system then retroactively creates the impression of conscious decision-making (Lau et al., 2007). When we examine the decisions we make each day, most of them are not the outcome of active deliberation. Our conscious experience of decision-making and action may not be as free and deliberate as we think.

Picture this: You accidently smash your finger with a hammer. Ouch! You pull your hand away and explain to yourself that you smashed your finger, it hurt, and then you pulled it away. But that is not exactly what happened. In reality, your finger had already moved before you even felt the pain. When you smash your finger, the pain receptors in your finger immediately send a signal to your spinal cord, which then sends a signal back to your finger to contract and pull away in a reflexive action. All of this happened before your brain even processed the pain signal and made you consciously aware of the pain. So your body moves first, and your brain catches up afterward. Here is the intriguing part: when your brain finally becomes conscious of the pain, it needs to make sense of what happened. Your brain fudges the timing and weaves together a story that fits with the idea that you consciously decided to move your finger because of the pain and that you have control over your actions.

There are distinct neural processes associated with the two types of decision-making: deliberative reasoning and intuitive decisions. Deliberative reasoning, characterized by cognitive control, deliberative reasoning, and mental effort, activates brain regions such as the middle frontal gyrus, the inferior parietal lobule, and the precuneus. On the other hand, intuitive decisions, driven by emotional processing and conflict detection, engage the insula and the anterior cingulate cortex (Kuo et al., 2009).

Another mechanism of intuitive decision-making is brain–gut interaction. When people say, "My gut tells me...," it is not just a figure of speech. They may be speaking it literally. Our gut, or enteric nervous system, sometimes referred to as the "second brain," communicates with our brain via the vagus nerve. Signals sent from the gut to the brain can influence feelings of danger or safety, which could be interpreted as a "gut feeling." If you have ever felt "butterflies" in your stomach when nervous, that is the gut–brain connection in action. Similarly, gut reactions to perceived danger – like a feeling in the pit of your stomach – are also related to this connection. Interoception is our ability to perceive and interpret internal body signals (Dunn et al., 2010). It plays a crucial role in shaping our emotions, decision-making, and sense of self. Interoception is closely tied to our experience of emotions. For example, our gut feelings can guide our decision-making based on somatic markers, signals sent from our body to our brain (Damasio, 1996). The insular cortex, a brain region involved in interoceptive processing, integrates and relays information about your internal body states to other areas responsible for emotions, cognition, and self-awareness (Critchley & Garfinkel, 2017).

The gut plays a significant role in shaping our decision-making processes through the use of neurotransmitters and signaling molecules. Take the neurotransmitter serotonin as an example. Surprisingly, around 95% of serotonin production occurs in our gut, not our brain. When serotonin levels are low, they are linked to impulsive behaviors and emotional instability. This is why serotonin is often seen as a mood stabilizer. However, an excess of serotonin can also harm both our body and brain, leading to feelings of agitation and restlessness. The brain–gut interaction is not only responsible for the maintenance of gastrointestinal homeostasis and digestion but also influences affect, motivation, and intuitive decision-making processes.

THE DOWNSIDES OF DELIBERATION

The two decision-making processes – intuitive decisions and deliberate decisions – often create a state of inner conflict where we have competing desires and are torn between different courses of action (Evans, 2008). Before we decide whether to trust our instincts, we need to be aware of the downsides of deliberation.

Deliberation promotes selfishness rather than cooperation (Rand et al., 2014). Cooperation is essential for social life because we cannot do everything on our own, but cooperation incurs individual costs. When engaging in cooperative behavior, we invest resources, time, or effort for the benefit of others, which may come at a cost to our own immediate interests. There is a risk of others taking advantage of our cooperative instinct. When we take time to think and deliberate, cooperation tends to decrease (Bear & Rand, 2016). On the other hand, our intuitive behavior tends to lead to cooperation, except under specific conditions where the cost of not receiving reciprocal cooperation is lower than the cost of cooperating unnecessarily. This helps explain why people still cooperate even in situations where interactions are anonymous and one-time (Fischbacher et al., 2001). In one-time anonymous interactions, if we encourage intuitive decision-making (by making deliberate thinking more difficult) as opposed to promoting deliberate thinking (by making it easier), we can anticipate an overall increase in cooperation. This is because people need to deliberate to realize that overriding their natural cooperative instinct is necessary (Delton et al., 2011; Rand et al., 2015).

Many moral decisions are made intuitively (Haidt, 2001). We have an innate sense of caring, kindness, and fairness that is part of our intuition (Van Berkum et al., 2009). Intuition is a better guide than deliberation to make moral decisions when conflicts of interest are involved (Fehr & Gächter, 2002), as deliberative analysis increases deception to maximize decision-makers' individual interests and reduces altruistic behaviors such as donating to a charity (Zhong, 2011). When decision-makers' self-interest and their group's collective interest were pitted against each other, the faster people decided, the more likely they were to put collective interest above individual interest (Rand et al., 2012).

WHEN SHOULD YOU TRUST YOUR INSTINCT?

Intuitive judgments are like the turbochargers of decision-making engines. They allow us to make quick decisions, but they also introduce errors. So when is it appropriate to trust our intuition? Intuition is more effective than deliberative analysis when you have a high level of domain expertise (Dane et al., 2012; Gigerenzer, 2007). When you are an expert in a particular field, your gut feeling becomes your trusty copilot, often outperforming lengthy analyses.

Experts store a significant amount of knowledge in their memories in chunks. They have around 50,000–200,000 "chunks" of familiar information about their field rather than an overwhelming 5,000,000 pieces of information stored by nonexperts. The chunks of knowledge are organized in memory through an "index," which helps distinguish between different stimuli. When an expert encounters a situation within their area of expertise, specific features or cues in that situation grab their attention. For example, a chess player immediately notices cues like "doubled pawns" or "pinned knights." Each recognized cue provides access to the relevant chunks of information stored in memory. The expert's ability to respond "intuitively," often swiftly and accurately, stems from their accumulated knowledge and their ability to solve problems through recognition. Intuition is essentially the ability to recognize and respond based on past experiences and acquired knowledge.

To identify if someone is an expert, we should not rely on self-acclaimed expertise but rather recognition from peers based on a track record of successful outcomes. As pointed out by Shanteau (1992), experts are *not* self-proclaimed gurus; they are the ones endorsed by their professional circles for consistently wielding the right skills at the right time. When your colleagues start saying things like, "If Person X was on the scene instead of Person Y, that task would not have spiraled out of control," you know you have earned your expert reputation in the group (Kahneman & Klein, 2009; Miller & Ireland, 2005).

The key takeaway is to be aware of the advantages and pitfalls of both deliberative and intuitive decision-making. Deliberation has its merits, but it can sometimes undermine cooperation and favor self-interest. Intuition, when guided by expertise, can be a powerful ally for quick and effective decision-making. Expertise, validated by successful outcomes and peer recognition, serves as a critical factor in the reliability of intuitive decisions.

11

BIASES: WHEN LEADERS' DECISION-MAKING GOES AWRY

Making intuitive decisions is fast. To do so, we take mental shortcuts that allow us to make decisions efficiently. Those mental shortcuts are called heuristics. They are intuitive, unconscious, rapid, and automatic, speeding up our decision-making process so fast that we sometimes cannot even articulate why we make a decision. Efficient decision-making powered by heuristics serves us well in daily life. When we see someone in danger and need help, we are likely to lend a helping hand – without a cost-benefit analysis. Walking into a social setting, we size up social dynamics within 40 milliseconds. In less than one-20th of a second, our brain processes nonverbal cues such as eye contact and body posture. Our brains then make a snap judgment of social hierarchy, such as who is dominant and who is subservient. Show us a human face, and our brains process the information about race within 100 milliseconds. About 50 milliseconds later, our brains process information about gender. Those mental processes take place so fast that we are not even sure we have seen something. By contrast, making a conscious decision is slow. To activate a conscious process that demands attention and working memory, it takes about 500 milliseconds (i.e., half a second).

But efficiency comes at a cost. To achieve speed in decision-making, decision quality may suffer. When heuristics go wrong, we make flawed decisions. Hiring managers evaluate the socioeconomic status of a job candidate almost as soon as the candidate begins speaking. Hiring managers take cues from the candidate's speech content – in some cases, only seven words. The hiring managers also take cues from pronunciation, tone, and rhythm. Unconsciously and inadvertently, the hiring managers may associate higher socioeconomic status with higher competency and a better fit for the job. This mental process can be characterized as a halo effect: people's tendency to like (or dislike) everything about a person – including things they have not observed. The halo effect in hiring decisions favors job applicants with higher socioeconomic status, perpetuating income inequality in society.

More importantly, heuristics do not just go wrong for one decision-maker randomly. Rather, they go wrong for most people, if not all of us. As a result, not only do people make mistakes, but they also make the same mistakes in a predictable way. The predictable, systematic errors in decision-making are called biases. They arise when people trade accuracy in decision-making for efficiency. Biases take place when people apply heuristics instinctively but inappropriately. Caution, therefore, must be exercised when we make decisions.

All humans carry biases, often at an unconscious level. Biases can consistently and predictably undermine our decisions. Leaders are expected to make data-informed, evidence-based decisions. Data, indeed, are like signposts. Without high-quality data, leaders are flying blind. Yet leaders often have to make decisions based on incomplete data, uncertainty, conflicting perspectives from stakeholders, unfamiliar team members, and time pressure in ever-changing, complex contexts. In fact, many decisions involve degrees of uncertainty that data-informed decision-making approaches are ill-equipped to handle. The rationality we think we bring to decision-making is often an illusion. To raise leaders' awareness of their decision errors, this chapter is followed by an introduction to three common biases in leaders' decision-making: (1) introspection illusion, (2) confirmation bias, and (3) in-group bias.

INTROSPECTION ILLUSION

Introspection is the process of examining our own conscious thoughts, emotions, motives, and intentions. Introspection illusion is our confident belief that we have direct access to our own mental processes and thoughts, and that we can accurately introspect or self-reflect on our own internal experiences. However, the majority of those mental processes remain largely unavailable for our conscious interpretation.

The information processing capacity of our conscious mind is estimated to be around 120 bits per second (Csikszentmihalyi & Nakamura, 2010). This capacity represents the maximum speed at which we can consciously process information at any given moment. In order for something to become part of our conscious experience, we need to consciously focus on it. However, a significant amount of information processing happens below the threshold of our conscious awareness. The catch is that we are unaware of our own lack of awareness. As a result, while introspection feels like we are simply observing our inner intentions, it is largely an inference about our intentions, rather than a true reflection of them. Moreover, we have exclusive access only to our own introspections and not those of others. This leads us to overestimate the value of our own introspective insights, adding another layer to the introspection illusion.

A decision we make can often be predicted even *before* we are consciously aware that we have made it. One decision-making process is called "gut feeling" or intuition, as introduced in the previous chapter. This process is like an internal compass, guiding us rapidly and primarily through nonconscious channels. It allows us to make decisions without an exhaustive search for information, evidence, or data. This intuitive process is a mental shortcut, fine-tuned through thousands of years of human history. Our ancestors, faced with immediate dangers and an urgent need to make fast decisions, have passed down this intuitive decision-making ability. Today, this intuitive process is at work in our everyday lives, driving our decisions on what to wear, what to eat, or even which route to take to work. It is a subconscious mental tool that is always in operation, silently guiding us through the many decisions we face every day.

What is even more interesting is how we rationalize our decisions after we have already made them. When asked to explain our decisions, our brains create post hoc or after-the-fact explanations. Those justifications "are all based on what makes it into our consciousness, but the reality is that the actions and the feelings happen before we are consciously aware of them – and most of them are the results of nonconscious processes, which will never make it into the explanations" (Gazzaniga, 2011, pp. 77–78).

Conscious rationalization, then, only has access to the information that has made its way into our conscious awareness. But in the complexity of the human brain, the subliminal state is a significantly robust part of the consciousness network. This means that no matter how hard we strive for self-understanding, certain mental and emotional processes are likely to remain subliminal, forever residing below the threshold of our conscious awareness. The vast depth of our minds remains a mystery to us.

When you claim that your decision-making process is objective and free from bias, you may be falling into the trap of the introspection illusion. It is like believing you hold the key to a secret vault in your mind, giving you full access to all your thoughts and motivations. But in reality, that is not the case. Given that our brains are naturally inclined to simplify complex decision-making processes, true "unbiased" decisions are essentially a myth. So, the notion of a completely unbiased decision is more of a mirage than a reality. Every decision we make is a colorful blend of mental shortcuts and past experiences, whether we are consciously aware of it or not. So, next time you are about to boast about your purely unbiased decisions, remember that even the best-intentioned choices carry traces of our biases and past experiences.

CONFIRMATION BIAS

Confirmation bias refers to our tendency to search for and interpret evidence in a way that validates a predetermined assumption or conclusion. We have a laser-sharp focus, selectively focusing on information that aligns with our views while conveniently sidestepping anything that challenges us. We see the world not as it is but as we want it to be. We see what we want to see.

Confirmation bias is like a personal cheerleader, encouraging us to give a standing ovation to information that supports our favored beliefs while booing and dismissing anything that dares to contradict us. It is a biased referee in the game of decision-making, unfairly favoring one team over the other. The result? Our decisions are skewed, not taking into account all the players on the field, especially those who do not align with our preconceived notions.

So, what happens in our brains when we favor information that reinforces our existing opinions and dismiss anything that contradicts them? It turns out that a region of our brain, the posterior medial prefrontal cortex, is the star of the show. This area, associated with memory, is like a diligent librarian, meticulously cataloging confirming information while relegating disconfirming information to the dusty, forgotten shelves of our minds.

When faced with disagreement, our brains do not just ignore opposing arguments. Instead, they are filed away on different shelves so we do not have to deal with it. It is not that our brains are oblivious to disconfirming information. Rather, the brain is quick to spot what we expect to see and slow to recognize what we do not. Our brains are masters of selective attention, adept at reinforcing our beliefs while shielding us from uncomfortable truths.

Remember, our brains are wired for energy efficiency. They are constantly trying to make sense of the world around us with the least amount of effort. This is where selective attention comes in. It is a mechanism that allows us to focus on information that we deem important while filtering out the rest. It is like a spotlight that illuminates only a portion of the stage, leaving the rest in darkness.

Now, when it comes to our beliefs, our brains have a vested interest in protecting them. Our beliefs form the foundation of our understanding of the world. They give us a sense of certainty and predictability, which are crucial for our survival. When those beliefs are challenged, it can create a sense of discomfort and uncertainty, something our brains naturally want to avoid. This is known as cognitive dissonance. To shield us from this discomfort, our brains selectively focus on information that aligns with our beliefs and downplay or ignore information that contradicts them. In doing so, our beliefs remain intact, and we are spared the discomfort of having to reassess our understanding of the world.

Moreover, our brains are not just passive recipients of information. They actively interpret and construct our reality based on our beliefs and expectations. This is known as top-down processing. When we receive new information, our brains do not just take it at face value. Instead, they interpret it in the context of our existing beliefs. If the new information fits neatly into our existing belief system, it is readily accepted. But if it contradicts our beliefs, our brains are likely to dismiss it or distort it in a way that makes it fit. This is how our brains reinforce our beliefs and shield us from uncomfortable truths because it helps maintain a sense of certainty and coherence in our understanding of the world. However, it also means that we need to be aware of the confirmation bias and make conscious efforts to challenge our beliefs and consider alternative perspectives.

A "safe space" can reinforce confirmation bias. Consider a group of like-minded people who find that they hold the same views. This mutual agreement can feel validating and comforting. However, it also reinforces their shared beliefs and makes them less likely to consider alternative viewpoints. Over time, the existing views become extreme as there is no one in the group to challenge or provide different perspectives.

Confirmation bias is prevalent. So here is the question: How can you effectively make your dissenting views heard? It is not as simple as bombarding others with counterevidence or shouting, "Data don't lie!" The human brain tends to dismiss contradictory information as categorically wrong, leaving us stuck in a dead-end alley. Merely repeating or yelling your dissenting views will not magically make people receptive to them. And throwing around statistics, graphs, and charts? That will not cut it either. The secret lies in finding a way to present disconfirming information in a format that others' brains can process. And how do we do that? By seeking common ground – the beliefs and values shared between you and your opposing party. When you tap into those shared beliefs and values, it triggers the brain's confirmation bias, making it more receptive to your perspective. Forget being hypercritical and nitpicking every flaw in others' arguments. Instead, focus on finding the common threads that bind you together. By highlighting shared beliefs and values, you create a foundation for meaningful and effective conversations.

So, if you truly want your dissenting views to be heard, remember this: it is not about overwhelming others with facts, data, and evidence. It is about finding common ground and engaging in a constructive dialogue that nurtures understanding. The purpose of communication is not to prove that "I'm right and you're wrong" but to have a better understanding and connection with others. It takes actively listening, exchanging ideas, and seeking common ground. By approaching communication with a genuine desire to understand others' perspectives and experiences, we can build bridges of understanding and make better decisions.

IN-GROUP BIAS

We usually favor and support groups to which we belong, particularly those that share our social identity. This creates a clear division between the "Us" (in-groups) and the "Them" (out-groups). This tendency is called in-group bias. Our brains process information in this way because it was efficient for our ancestors to process information in an environment where interacting with people from their own tribes or close communities was the norm. This process is called categorization.

Categorization means grouping similar items together, much like sorting items into folders. It is not a malicious trait of our minds but rather a practical strategy. The reason behind categorization lies in energy conservation, which is crucial for our survival. Our brains constantly face an overwhelming amount of information from the world around us. By categorizing people into "Us" (in-groups) and "Them" (out-groups) based on shared social identities, we can streamline the way we process information and make decisions. This streamlined approach saves cognitive resources and reduces the mental load caused by the constant stimuli bombarding us. Through this process of categorization, our brains can rely on seemingly predictable patterns and familiar associations. As a result, decision-making becomes more efficient and faster, which is highly beneficial in situations where quick judgments and actions are necessary for survival and well-being.

Our brains are remarkably efficient when it comes to processing social information. In the blink of an eye, in only 150 milliseconds (about one-tenth of a second), we determine the gender of a person by looking at their face.

During this same rapid timeframe, we are also able to gauge the person's social status. This ability to quickly categorize individuals into different groups based on gender and social standing is a fundamental aspect of human social cognition. It likely served as an adaptive mechanism for our ancestors when navigating complex social environments.

While our brains are wired to categorize people based on social groups, we no longer live in the simple tribal communities of the past. In today's diverse and interconnected world, we have many layers of identities. However, our brains have not fully adapted to those changes in our environment. The mental process of categorization can sometimes make us treat people differently based on whether they belong to our in-group or out-group. Unfortunately, this can undermine our efforts to understand out-group members. Instead of embracing diverse perspectives, our in-group bias undermines genuine connections and our ability to empathize with those who are in our out-groups.

Whenever we use labels to categorize people into groups, we create a division between "Us" and "Them." In-groups are seen as allies, while out-groups are considered adversaries. Our brains rapidly distinguish between friends and foes in order to identify potential threats. Much like a smoke detector, our brain's threat-detection system frequently registers false alarms to avoid overlooking a threat. Similarly, faces from out-groups can trigger our brain's threat-detection system, even in the absence of danger. If you were alone in a dimly lit alley at night and a man suddenly appeared from a doorway, your brain would categorize him based on sensory cues within fractions of a second, triggering feelings of fear and preparing your body to respond. In experiments in Canada, researchers manipulated participants to feel either more fearful or confident in the dark alley scenario. The findings showed that Canadian participants rated Iraqis as less trustworthy and more hostile than their fellow Canadians, reflecting the influence of in-group bias on their perceptions. White participants were more likely to misinterpret anger on the faces of Black men than white men after watching a terrifying scene from the psychological horror film "The Silence of the Lambs" (Culotta, 2012). This suggests that the heightened emotional response due to fear influences how the research participants perceive members of out-groups, leading to potential misunderstandings and biased judgments.

The Olympics aspire to promote global peace and unity through sports. However, this event not only triggers national identity but also underscores fierce rivalries between nations. As a result, during the Olympics, people tend to exhibit increased in-group bias and have more negative attitudes toward out-groups. A research study showed that during the Olympics, Koreans were less willing to donate to help migrant workers and showed a tendency to discriminate against Southeast Asian job applicants. Another finding was that those negative attitudes were prominent for negatively stereotyped out-groups (such as Southeast Asians and Chinese) but not for favorably stereotyped out-groups (like Canadians; Kim & Na, 2020).

A heightened sense of in-group versus out-group undermines unity, turning potential opportunities for intergroup understanding into points of conflict. So, how can we engage with out-groups to ease tension and prejudice? First, it is important to identify and cultivate a shared identity – a collective sense of "us." For example, astronauts aboard the International Space Station embrace the common identity of being "astronauts" rather than defining themselves by their nationalities. This collective identity is nurtured through shared experiences and regular intergroup interactions within the confines of the space station.

Second, fair treatment of all groups is not only an ethical imperative but also a key factor in maximizing the advantages of diversity. Research indicates a positive correlation between fair treatment and self-reported happiness. Brain imaging studies have demonstrated that fair treatment activates the dopaminergic reward system, leading to feelings of satisfaction and contentment. On the other hand, unfair treatment triggers negative emotions, especially anger, motivating people to react strongly against such injustices (Sanfey et al., 2003). That innate sense of justice within us compels us to challenge and reject injustices. Promoting fairness in all aspects of society not only improves overall well-being but also strengthens social cohesion and harmony.

Third, intergroup contact can be a powerful tool to counteract in-group bias and capitalize on the benefits of diversity. In a study of 22 years of worldwide data, researchers showed that when society encountered diversity, people initially reacted negatively to threats of disrupting homogeneity. However, the negative effects of diversity were compensated in the long run through the positive outcomes of intergroup contact. As people engage and interact with members of different groups, they see beyond stereotypes and develop a more inclusive perspective, which reshapes their broader social identity and mitigates the in-group bias. By promoting meaningful interactions between diverse groups, we can transcend initial barriers and build bridges of understanding, leading to a more united and cohesive society.

Take a moment and think about your close friends – the ones you feel comfortable sharing your inner thoughts with. Do you notice any patterns in their social identity, such as gender, race, ethnicity, political affiliation, or religion? If you find that your close friends mostly share your social identity, it is time to reach out and get to know people who do not share the same background as you. Consider forming connections with people from diverse backgrounds and getting to know them on a more intimate and personal level. Building relationships with people who have different perspectives and experiences can enrich and broaden your understanding of the world. Embracing diversity in your social circle can lead to greater empathy, respect, and a more inclusive worldview. Take it one step at a time, creating and strengthening one intergroup social tie at a time.

In a world that is growing more diverse and interconnected, it is more important than ever that we acknowledge in-group bias and strive to mitigate it. Like astronauts on the International Space Station who embrace their collective identity over nationalities, we too can shape our shared identity in this global village. Remember, in the grand scheme of things, we are all part of one big in-group called humanity.

12

BRAIN-TO-BRAIN SYNCHRONY IN COLLECTIVE DECISION-MAKING

All previous chapters focused on leaders' decision-making as individuals. But studying a single person's brain is not enough to fully understand social behaviors. In this chapter, we will explore how leaders can facilitate high-quality collective decision-making. One may wonder: How does a collective mind emerge from a group of individual minds? How do organizational structure, rules, and policies work against harnessing the collective wisdom of collective decision-making? Asking a group to make a decision does not necessarily ensure high decision quality. If an organization is not instrumental in generating collective wisdom, collective decision-making produces lower quality decisions than individual decision-making, as stated in Condorcet's jury theorem. This chapter introduces brain-to-brain synchrony that takes place in collective decision-making and how leaders can create an organization that promotes brain-to-brain synchrony.

BRAIN-TO-BRAIN SYNCHRONIZATION AS AN ENERGY-EFFICIENT SOLUTION

Our brains have regular fluctuations in the electrical or biochemical signals generated by groups of neurons. Neurons have specialized structures called dendrites and axons. Dendrites receive signals from other neurons, while axons transmit signals to other neurons. Neurons communicate with each other through electrical impulses known as action potentials. The synchronized activity of neurons occurs through a combination of excitatory and inhibitory inputs. Excitatory signals increase the likelihood of a neuron firing an action potential, while inhibitory signals decrease this likelihood. The balance between excitatory and inhibitory inputs determines whether a group of neurons will fire together or not.

When large groups of neurons synchronize their activity, it results in the production of brain waves. The frequency of brain waves corresponds to the rate at which neurons fire action potentials. Imagine a symphony playing inside your brain, even when you are not doing anything. Scientists have discovered that distant regions of the brain dance together, creating mesmerizing patterns of synchronized activity. This phenomenon, seen in humans, monkeys, and rodents, is like the resonance modes of musical instruments, producing echoes and reverberations. Each brain region has its own unique rhythm, contributing to the symphony of brain activity (Cabral et al., 2023). The harmonious waves are crucial for normal brain function, orchestrating coordinated activity. The rhythmic and repetitive patterns of neural activity are called brain oscillations. They are believed to coordinate and synchronize neural activity across different brain regions, allowing for effective communication and information integration. They provide a temporal framework for coordinating the flow of information and facilitating the coordination of neuronal ensembles involved in specific tasks or cognitive operations.

When we engage in social interactions, such as between infants and adults, conversations, working with others, or even observing each other's behavior, our brain activity can synchronize with others' brains (Kawasaki et al., 2013; Piazza et al., 2020). This phenomenon is called brain-to-brain synchrony. It refers to coordinated activity or the synchronization of neural activity between different individuals. Brain-to-brain synchrony facilitates communication, understanding, and alignment between different people as their brains exhibit similar patterns of activity. By synchronizing their brain activities, we develop a shared understanding or mental representation of social information. This alignment of neural processes can influence an individual's thoughts, attitudes, and behaviors as they become attuned to the social cues and information present in the interaction. The brain-to-brain synchrony is especially strong when we direct our gaze toward our teammates' face (Hirsch et al., 2017). Our brains are on the same wavelength, collectively navigating the challenges at hand. In this "we-mode," different human brains share cognition and seamlessly interact with others. When brains are synchronized, people in a group are more likely to be "on the same page" – meaning that they are thinking along similar lines, interpreting information in a similar way, and likely to reach similar conclusions. Synchronized brains reduce the frequency of misunderstandings, leading to smoother interactions and lower cognitive effort for each individual. Brain-to-brain synchrony also helps align people's attention and focus on shared goals, reducing the mental effort needed to coordinate tasks and make collective decisions. On the other hand, when we work individually, within-brain synchronization becomes more prominent. Our brain focuses on its own internal processes without the need to align with others. It is like a switch that flips when you shift from cooperation to independent work (Xu et al., 2023).

To meet our brains' high energy demand, our brains secretly work with other brains (Bilek et al., 2015). When we are with someone we care about, our brain activities synchronize. If our loved one is in pain, we can lessen their suffering merely by holding their hand (Guastello et al., 2017). Being a social species has all sorts of advantages for us. One advantage is that we live longer if we have close, supportive relationships with other people. It may seem obvious that loving relationships are good for us, but studies show that the benefits go beyond what common sense would suggest. If you and your partner feel that your relationship is intimate and caring, that you are responsive to each other's needs, and that life seems easy and enjoyable when you are together, both of you are less likely to get sick. If you are already sick with a serious illness, such as cancer or heart disease, you are more likely to get better. These studies were conducted on married couples, but the results appear to hold for close friendships too, and even for pet owners. On the other hand, some people can be a source of stress, draining our limited brain energy. When we do not trust each other, our brains are like dance partners who step on each other's toes. If I raise my voice, or even my eyebrow, I can affect what goes on inside other people's bodies, such as their heart rate or the chemicals carried in their bloodstream. If your supervisor abuses their power by wrongly accusing you of insubordination as a threat to you, odds are that it will affect your nervous system in an unpleasant way.

LEADING AND FOLLOWING IN SYNC

In effective teams, leaders and followers' brain activities sync up. We often mirror others' movements unknowingly. That process is choreographed by our brains. One of us leads, the other follows, and sometimes we switch. Both leading and following require social awareness and mutual adaptation between leader and follower, but there are differences. Leading is more socially focused and involves empathy, sharing of feelings, and social engagement. Following, on the other hand, has more motoric and temporally related neural reactivity (Silfwerbrand et al., 2023). These differences indicate that leading is not just barking orders and commands; it also requires understanding followers' needs, taking their perspectives, and sharing their feelings. Leaders who do this can synchronize and join actions with their followers, leading to better teamwork and overall performance.

In group discussions that lead to collective decision-making, leadership emerges from the brain synchronization between leaders and followers, as well as among followers (Jiang et al., 2015). To synchronize brain activities, leaders' role is not to make individual decisions or make their personal preferences known to the group before the group discussion starts. Instead, leaders' roles shift to ensure the group makes quality decisions. To do so, leaders guide group discussions and deliberations by initiating high-quality social interactions in which leaders capitalize on the skills of understanding others' mental states, such as feelings and intentions, express positive emotions toward the group members, encourage group members to engage in divergent thinking, and ultimately reach the stage of brain synchronization.

CREATE AN ORGANIZATION THAT PROMOTES BRAIN-TO-BRAIN SYNCHRONY

Leaders' role in collective decision-making is not to make decisions as individuals. If that were the case, there would be no need for a group to engage in the decision-making process. Instead, the leaders' role is to ensure that a group collectively makes high-quality decisions. Leaders can achieve this by creating an environment that fosters brain-to-brain synchrony. The synchronization can be facilitated by focusing on three key components of the collective decision-making process: (1) a wide variance of viewpoints in the group, (2) group's size, and (3) rules used to aggregate individual preferences into a collective decision. By paying attention to these aspects, leaders can steer the group toward high-quality decisions.

Variance of Viewpoints

Decision-making is to choose a course of action out of a choice set. A main benefit of making decisions as a group is that multiple group members are expected to enlarge the choice set by bringing different perspectives and ideas, which engage different cognitive functions. For example, a creative idea activates brain regions related to imagination and abstract thinking, while a data-driven opinion stimulates analytical areas of the brain. Leaders must facilitate a process where the diverse neural activations are synchronized, enabling a coherent and collective understanding.

To do so, leaders can use empathy to promote emotional resonance and perspective-taking. Empathy means taking others' perspective and feeling what another person is feeling.

In a group with diverse viewpoints, leaders can encourage active listening by paying full attention, asking questions, and reflecting on what has been said. By genuinely listening to others, group members can better understand different viewpoints. This understanding through empathy can lead to synchronized neural activity in brain regions like the insula and anterior cingulate cortex (Singer et al., 2004).

Moreover, nonverbal communication, such as facial expression, gestures, and eye contact, can also facilitate brain-to-brain synchrony. Nonverbal cues such as facial expressions, body language, and hand gestures can evoke shared neural experiences. For example, a smile or a nod may activate mirror neurons – the specialized neurons that activate not only when a person performs a specific action but also when they observe another person engaging in the same action. When we observe someone else yawning, mirror neurons in our brain can become activated, leading to the initiation of our own yawning. The mirror neurons play an essential role in our capacity for empathy and the shared experiences we encounter with others (Rizzolatti & Sinigaglia, 2010). Sustained eye contact is another powerful nonverbal cue that can lead to brain-to-brain synchrony, fostering trust and rapport among group members (Hietanen et al., 2018).

A caveat is that leaders should refrain from sharing their opinions at the start of collective decision-making. Leaders often hold a unique position of authority and influence within a group, and their opinions carry substantial weight. If a leader shares their opinion early, it may unintentionally guide or bias the thinking of other group members. Team members may conform to the leader's views rather than contribute unique perspectives. This conformity might lead to superficial alignment in thinking but can suppress brain-to-brain synchrony based on diverse viewpoints, not merely group members mirroring leaders' viewpoints.

Group Size

A large group can offer a wide range of viewpoints, thereby enlarging the choice set for collective decision-making. However, an excessively large group can disrupt brain-to-brain synchrony due to increased complexity in interactions and cognitive overload. Leaders should be cautious not to over-whelm team members in large groups, which can lead to a lack of clarity and alignment in decision-making (Navajas et al., 2018). For transparency, it is tempting to be inclusive and invite more people than necessary to make a group decision. Sometimes, having more people in a group does not increase the quality of a group decision, but it does require more effort in communi-cation and coordination. An optimal group size, typically ranging from five to seven members, can facilitate more focused discussions and more synchronized brain activity (Kao & Couzin, 2014).

Collective Decision-making Procedures

Collective decision-making can go wrong if the individual group member's preference aggregation rule is ill-defined and not agreed upon prior to decision-making. An important task for leaders in collective decision-making is to develop clear procedures for aggregating individual group member's pref-erences. Whether group decisions are made unanimously or by majority vote can significantly influence outcomes (Miller, 1985). So do plurality voting (i.e., the highest number of votes wins) or ranked choice voting (i.e., voters rank candidates in order of preference; Johnson et al., 2022). The absence of well-defined and agreed-upon decision-making rules can lead to confusion, frustration, and a lack of trust in a group. Consider a situation where a leader's proposal is unanimously rejected by the team. In this case, an agreed-upon decision-making rule prior to decision-making about whether a leader has the power to overrule the group can create clarity and alignment. Such clarity creates shared understanding, aligning neural pathways that facilitate communication.

13

CARE FOR OUR BRAINS TO MAKE BETTER DECISIONS

Our brain is an organ that makes decisions. When we neglect our decision-making organ, we make subpar decisions. This is similar to why we take care of our cars. If we fail to do so, our car may break down on the road or we may lose control, causing it to run into ditches. To make wise decisions, leaders must take care of their decision-making organs – their brains. More importantly, it is insufficient for leaders to focus solely on their own brains. Leaders must also take care of the brains of their team members. Each organizational member is akin to a neuron in the human brain. Organizational members receive and process information before deciding whether to send it to the next neuron. One organizational member may relay one piece of information to the next, but another member, for whatever reasons, may decide to withhold the information. In this case, leaders are not the only members of great importance in an organization. Rather, each organizational member performs their duties in an organization, just as each neuron performs its function in the human brain. This chapter introduces five ways that leaders can follow to maintain optimal brain health: food for thought, physical exercise, cognitive stimulation, social engagement, and stress management.

FOOD FOR THOUGHT

Proper nutrition is essential for maintaining healthy brain function. Just as a car needs high-quality fuel to operate optimally, the brain requires a balanced diet to operate at its peak. Leaders who nourish their brains with the right nutrients can optimize their cognitive abilities, allowing for better decision-making. This includes eating foods abundant in vitamins, minerals, and antioxidants that protect brain cells. Similarly, encouraging team members to adhere to a healthy diet can improve the overall functioning of the organization's "neurons," thereby nurturing a more effective and cohesive decision-making process.

PHYSICAL EXERCISE

Regular physical activity strengthens the heart and lungs, which has a profound impact on increasing brain blood flow. With improved blood circulation, the brain receives more oxygen and nutrients, which improve cognitive functions and enable better decision-making. Leaders who engage in activities that increase their heart rate are able to think more clearly, approach problems creatively, and make decisions more efficiently.

Exercise is not merely a tool for physical fitness; it also unlocks enhanced memory and learning capabilities. The hippocampus, a brain region that plays a crucial role in memory and learning, shrinks in late adulthood. Even in old age, exercise training increases the size of the hippocampus, improving memory, processing speed, and executive function of the brain. Aerobic exercises, strength training, and even stretching have all been shown to increase the size of key memory-related brain regions (Erickson et al., 2011). In leadership positions where critical thinking and timely decision-making are demanded, mental acuity and clarity are pivotal. Regular exercise improves mental acuity by stimulating the release of neurotransmitters (e.g., dopamine and serotonin) that enhance the structure and function of neurons. Coordination and balance exercises, for example, are excellent activities for maintaining and enhancing mental sharpness (Voelcker-Rehage & Niemann, 2013).

Leaders frequently experience elevated levels of stress, which can impair their ability to make high-quality decisions. Exercise not only lowers the levels of stress hormones such as adrenaline and cortisol but also stimulates the production of endorphins, the body's natural mood boosters. Maintaining a regular exercise routine can thus help leaders manage stress better, allowing them to approach decisions with a calm and focused mind.

Creating an organizational culture that values physical fitness has advantages beyond personal benefits. When leaders encourage and provide opportunities for team members to engage in physical activity, they contribute to a healthier, more vibrant working environment. This not only promotes individual well-being but also collectively creates a more agile and responsive brain at the organizational level. Healthy employees are typically more productive and engaged, which can lead to more creative and effective decision-making.

COGNITIVE STIMULATION

Physical exercise is essential for body health, and mental exercise plays a similar role for brain health. Engaging the mind keeps it sharp and active, thereby supporting cognitive functions that are vital for leaders' decision-making. The principle of "use it or lose it" emphasizes that mental faculties can deteriorate if not regularly challenged. Novel, challenging, and complex activities are an effective method for cognitive training. Whether it is solving intricate puzzles, pursuing advanced courses in unfamiliar subjects, or engaging in strategic games like chess, all of those activities push your brain to adapt and grow.

Acquiring a new language not only enriches communication skills but also strengthens cognitive muscles. It engages memory, attention, and comprehension, strengthening the brain's ability to process information (Veroude et al., 2010). This skill can be particularly beneficial for leaders operating in global environments. Mastering a musical instrument requires coordination, concentration, and imagination. It is an engaging way to challenge multiple brain regions and promote cognitive flexibility. In addition, training yourself to use your nondominant hand for daily tasks forces the brain to form new neural pathways and connections. This practice promotes cognitive resilience and adaptability, both of which are valuable in leadership roles.

Leaders can also create an organizational culture that encourages continuous learning and intellectual curiosity. By providing opportunities for professional development, hosting workshops, and encouraging creative problem-solving, leaders build a team that is agile, innovative, and prepared to face new challenges.

SOCIAL ENGAGEMENT

Social engagement is not only a source of delight and companionship but also plays a fundamental role in emotional well-being and cognitive health. Leadership, by its nature, is a social process. Engaging in social activities and building strong relationships has a direct impact on leaders' decision-making abilities. By creating a culture where every team member feels valued and appreciated, leaders encourage collaboration and innovation. This environment encourages the free flow of ideas, resulting in well-informed decisions. Intergroup communication is the exchange of information and ideas between different groups or teams. This level of communication breaks down silos and promotes a unified approach to problem-solving.

To build trust, leaders must invest time in getting to know their team members and gaining an understanding of their needs and aspirations. Strong relationships facilitate collaboration, leading to better alignment and more effective decision-making processes. Regular meetings encourage open communication, allow for the exchange of ideas, and provide a platform for collaborative problem-solving. Organizing social events and team-building activities promotes camaraderie and a sense of belonging, which are necessary for a cohesive and productive team.

STRESS MANAGEMENT

Stress is an everyday occurrence, but when it becomes chronic, it poses a serious threat to our health and our ability to make sound decisions. The effects of chronic stress on the brain can be devastating. There are three types of workplace stressors. First, individual stressors refer to relationships with coworkers, supervisors, or leaders that can create stress. Whether it is a challenging personality or incompatible work styles, individual interactions can result in ongoing tension. Second, when our roles and responsibilities do not align with our skills and personalities, the mismatch can create a constant source of stress. Third, changes in policies, procedures, protocols, and personnel can disrupt the stability of our work environment, causing anxiety and unease.

Unlike acute stress, which is a short-lived reaction to a specific event, chronic stress persists for extended periods. Its impact on the brain is alarming. Chronic stress affects brain regions associated with emotion regulation, resulting in heightened sensitivity to negative emotions and a diminished ability to handle challenging situations. Chronic stress also influences decision-making abilities by disrupting the serotonin and dopamine systems, which are essential for sound judgment and problem-solving. The persistent release of stress hormones such as cortisol can cause structural changes in brain regions such as the amygdala and hippocampus, which are vital for stress regulation and emotional processing (Thomas et al., 2007). This can exacerbate anxiety, depression, and other mental health conditions.

In the workplace, chronic stressors manifest in different forms. Role ambiguity means unclear job responsibilities or expectations, which can leave us feeling lost and unsupported. Likewise, lack of control is a chronic stressor. Feeling powerless over work tasks and the environment can erode confidence and well-being. An abusive supervisor creates a hostile or demeaning environment that functions as a chronic stressor. Those stressors cause an increase in heart rate, blood pressure, and respiration rate, preparing the body for "fight or flight." By identifying the signs and sources of chronic stress, leaders can create a supportive and resilient work environment. Encouraging open communication, providing clear expectations, and promoting work–life balance are strategies that can mitigate chronic stress.

In concluding this journey through neuroscience and leaders' decision-making, it becomes evident that our human brain is not only a biological organ but also a complex decision-making organ. This book not only introduces neuroscience related to leaders' decision-making but also offers applicable practices leaders can follow in both their professional and personal lives. Remember that effective leadership requires not only mastery of external skills and strategies but also an understanding of the internal neural mechanisms that influence your behavior and decision-making abilities. Neuroscience provides us with the means to enhance these internal processes, which not only makes us better leaders but also more well-rounded people. Thank you for joining this illuminating journey. May the knowledge in this book serve you well in your endeavors as a leader.

REFERENCES

Acton JEED. (1887/[1972]). Letter to Mandell Creighton, April 5, 1887. In G. Himmelfarb (Ed.), *Essays on freedom and power* (pp. 335–336). Smith.

Adams, J. (1772). *Oration at Braintree*. National Archives. https://founders.archives.gov/documents/Adams/01-02-02-0002-0002-0001

Allee, W. C., Collias, N. E., & Lutherman, C. Z. (1939). Modification of the social order in flocks of hens by the injection of testosterone propionate. *Physiological Zoology, 12*(4), 412–440.

Alrajih, S., & Ward, J. (2014). Increased facial width-to-height ratio and perceived dominance in the faces of the UK's leading business leaders. *British Journal of Psychology, 105*(2), 153–161.

Amodio, D. M., Shah, J. Y., Sigelman, J., Brazy, P. C., & Harmon-Jones, E. (2004). Implicit regulatory focus associated with asymmetrical frontal cortical activity. *Journal of Experimental Social Psychology, 40*(2), 225–232.

Anderson, C., & Galinsky, A. D. (2006). Power, optimism, and risk-taking. *European Journal of Social Psychology, 36*(4), 511–536.

Andreoni, J. (1988). Why free ride? Strategies and learning in public goods experiments. *Journal of Public Economics, 37*(3), 291–304.

Archer, J. (2006). Testosterone and human aggression: An evaluation of the challenge hypothesis. *Neuroscience & Biobehavioral Reviews, 30*(3), 319–345.

Arvey, R. D., Rotundo, M., Johnson, W., Zhang, Z., & McGue, M. (2006). The determinants of leadership role occupancy: Genetic and personality factors. *The Leadership Quarterly, 17*(1), 1–20.

Arvey, R. D., Zhang, Z., Avolio, B. J., & Krueger, R. F. (2007). Developmental and genetic determinants of leadership role occupancy among women. *Journal of Applied Psychology, 92*(3), 693–706.

Atkinson, A. P., & Adolphs, R. (2011). The neuropsychology of face perception: Beyond simple dissociations and functional selectivity. *Philosophical Transactions of the Royal Society B: Biological Sciences*, *366*(1571), 1726–1738.

Babiak, P., Neumann, C. S., & Hare, R. D. (2010). Corporate psychopathy: Talking the walk. *Behavioral Sciences & the Law*, *28*(2), 174–193.

Bacanli, F. (2006). Personality characteristics as predictors of personal indecisiveness. *Journal of Career Development*, *32*(4), 320–332.

Bagozzi, R. P., Verbeke, W. J. M. I., Dietvorst, R. C., Belschak, F. D., van den Berg, W. E., & Rietdijk, W. J. R. (2013). Theory of mind and empathic explanations of Machiavellianism: A neuroscience perspective. *Journal of Management*, *39*, 1760–1798.

Bailenson, J. N., Iyengar, S., Yee, N., & Collins, N. A. (2008). Facial similarity between voters and candidates causes influence. *Public Opinion Quarterly*, *72*(5), 935–961.

Ballew, C. C., & Todorov, A. (2007). Predicting political elections from rapid and unreflective face judgments. *Proceedings of the National Academy of Sciences*, *104*(46), 17948–17953.

Barrett, L. F. (2017). *How emotions are made: The secret life of the brain*. Houghton Mifflin Harcourt.

Bartra, O., McGuire, J. T., & Kable, J. W. (2013). The valuation system: A coordinate-based meta-analysis of BOLD fMRI experiments examining neural correlates of subjective value. *NeuroImage*, *76*, 412–427.

Bear, A., & Rand, D. G. (2016). Intuition, deliberation, and the evolution of cooperation. *Proceedings of the National Academy of Sciences*, *113*(4), 936–941.

Bechara, A. (2004). The role of emotion in decision-making: Evidence from neurological patients with orbitofrontal damage. *Brian and Cognition*, *55*(1), 30–40.

Belli, R. F., Lindsay, D. S., Gales, M. S., & McCarthy, T. T. (1994). Memory impairment and source misattribution in postevent misinformation experiments with short retention intervals. *Memory & Cognition*, *22*, 40–54.

Bénabou, R., & Tirole, J. (2002). Self-confidence and personal motivation. *Quarterly Journal of Economics*, *117*(3), 871–915.

Bernston, G. G., Bechara, A., Damasio, H., Tranel, D., & Cacioppo, J. T. (2007). Amygdala contribution to selective dimensions of emotion. *Social Cognitive and Affective Neuroscience, 2*(2), 123–129.

Bilek, E., Ruf, M., Schäfer, A., Akdeniz, C., Calhoun, V. D., Schmahl, C., ... Meyer-Lindenberg, A. (2015). Information flow between interacting human brains: Identification, validation, and relationship to social expertise. *Proceedings of the National Academy of Sciences, 112*(16), 5207–5212.

Blair, R. J. (2010). Neuroimaging of psychopathy and antisocial behavior: A targeted review. *Current Psychiatry Reports, 12*, 76–82.

Boddy, C. R. (2015). Psychopathic leadership a case study of a corporate psychopath CEO. *Journal of Business Ethics, 145*(1), 141–156.

Booth, A., Shelley, G., Mazur, A., Tharp, G., & Kittok, R. (1989). Testosterone, and winning and losing in human competition. *Hormones and Behavior, 23*(4), 556–571.

Borkenau, P., Brecke, S., Möttig, C., & Paelecke, M. (2009). Extraversion is accurately perceived after a 50-ms exposure to a face. *Journal of Research in Personality, 43*(4), 703–706.

Boyatzis, R. E., Passarelli, A. M., Koenig, K., Lowe, M., Matthew, B., Stoller, J. K., & Phillips, M. (2012). Examination of the neural substrates activated in memories of experiences with resonant and dissonant leaders. *The Leadership Quarterly, 23*(2), 259–272.

Brooks, M. E. (2011). Management indecision. *Management Decision, 49*(5), 683–693.

Bugental, D. B., & Lewis, J. C. (1999). The paradoxical misuse of power by those who see themselves as powerless: How does it happen? *Journal of Social Issues, 55*, 51–64.

Burgess, P. W. (2000). Strategy application disorder: The role of the frontal lobes in human multitasking. *Psychological Research, 63*(3–4), 279–288.

Buyl, T., Boone, C., & Wade, J. B. (2017). CEO narcissism, risk-taking, and resilience: An empirical analysis in US commercial banks. *Journal of Management, 45*(4), 1372–1400.

Cabral, J., Fernandes, F. F., & Shemesh, N. (2023). Intrinsic macroscale oscillatory modes driving long range functional connectivity in female rat brains detected by ultrafast fMRI. *Nature Communications, 14*(1). Article Number 375.

Carré, J. M., McCormick, C. M., & Mondloch, C. J. (2009). Facial structure is a reliable cue of aggressive behavior. *Psychological Science, 20*(10), 1194–1198.

Cassia, V. M., Picozzi, M., Kuefner, D., & Casati, M. (2009). Short article: Why mix-ups don't happen in the nursery: Evidence for an experience-based interpretation of the other-age effect. *Quarterly Journal of Experimental Psychology, 62*(6), 1099–1107.

Chen, S., Lee Chai, A. Y., & Bargh, J. A. (2001). Relationship orientation as a moderator of the effects of social power. *Journal of Personality and Social Psychology, 80*, 173–187.

Chew, S. H., Huang, W., & Zhao, X. (2020). Motivated false memory. *Journal of Political Economy, 128*(10), 3913–3939.

Chinta, S. J., & Andersen, J. K. (2005). Dopaminergic neurons. *The International Journal of Biochemistry & Cell Biology, 37*(5), 942–946.

Chong, T. J., Bonnelle, V., & Husain, M. (2016). Quantifying motivation with effort-based decision-making paradigms in health and disease. In *Progress in brain research* (Vol. 229, pp. 71–100). Elsevier.

Costa, M., Lio, G., Gomez, A., & Sirigu, A. (2017). How components of facial width to height ratio differently contribute to the perception of social traits. *PLoS One, 12*(2), e0172739.

Cowen, A. S., & Keltner, D. (2020). What the face displays: Mapping 28 emotions conveyed by naturalistic expression. *American Psychologist, 75*(3), 349–364.

Critchley, H. D., & Garfinkel, S. N. (2017). Interoception and emotion. *Current Opinion in Psychology, 17*, 7–14.

Crockett, M. J. (2009). The neurochemistry of fairness clarifying the link between serotonin and prosocial behavior. *Annals of the New York Academy of Sciences, 1167*(1), 76–86.

Csikszentmihalyi, M., & Nakamura, J. (2010). Effortless attention in everyday life: A systematic phenomenology. In B. Bruya (Ed.), *Effortless attention: A new perspective in the cognitive science of attention and action* (pp. 179–190). MIT Press.

Culotta, E. (2012). Roots of racism. *Science, 336*(6083), 825–827.

Dabbs, J. M., Jr. (1992). Testosterone and occupational achievement. *Social Forces, 70*(3), 813–824.

Damasio, A. R. (1996). The somatic marker hypothesis and the possible functions of the prefrontal cortex. *Philosophical Transactions of the Royal Society of London. Series B: Biological Sciences, 351*(1346), 1413–1420.

Damasio, A., & Carvalho, G. B. (2013). The nature of feelings: Evolutionary and neurobiological origins. *Nature Reviews Neuroscience, 14*, 143–152.

Dane, E., & Pratt, M. G. (2007). Exploring intuition and its role in managerial decision making. *Academy of Management Review, 32*(1), 33–54.

Dane, E., Rockmann, K. W., & Pratt, M. G. (2012). When should I trust my gut? Linking domain expertise to intuitive decision-making effectiveness. *Organizational Behavior and Human Decision Processes, 119*(2), 187–194.

De Dreu, C. K., Greer, L. L., Handgraaf, M. J., Shalvi, S., Van Kleef, G. A., Baas, M., ... Feith, S. W. (2010). The neuropeptide oxytocin regulates parochial altruism in intergroup conflict among humans. *Science, 328*(5984), 1408–1411.

De Dreu, C. K., Greer, L. L., Van Kleef, G. A., Shalvi, S., & Handgraaf, M. J. (2011). Oxytocin promotes human ethnocentrism. *Proceedings of the National Academy of Sciences, 108*(4), 1262–1266.

De Gelder, B., & Vroomen, J. (2000). The perception of emotions by ear and by eye. *Cognition & Emotion, 14*(3), 289–311.

De Waal, F. (2019). *Mama's last hug: Animal and human emotions.* W. W. Norton & Company.

Decety, J., & Cacioppo, S. (2012). The speed of morality: A high-density electrical neuroimaging study. *Journal of Neurophysiology, 108*(11), 3068–3072.

Decety, J., Chen, C., Harenski, C., & Kiehl, K. A. (2013). An fMRI study of affective perspective taking in individuals with psychopathy: Imagining another in pain does not evoke empathy. *Frontiers in Human Neuroscience, 7.* https://doi.org/10.3389/fnhum.2013.00489. Article 489.

Decety, J., & Yoder, K. J. (2017). The emerging social neuroscience of justice motivation. *Trends in Cognitive Sciences, 21*(4), 6–14.

Dekkers, T. J., van Rentergem, J. A. A., Meijer, B., Popma, A., Wagemaker, E., & Huizenga, H. M. (2019). A meta-analytical evaluation of the dual-hormone hypothesis: Does cortisol moderate the relationship between testosterone and status, dominance, risk taking, aggression, and psychopathy? *Neuroscience & Biobehavioral Reviews, 96*, 250–271.

Delton, A. W., Krasnow, M. M., Cosmides, L., & Tooby, J. (2011). Evolution of direct reciprocity under uncertainty can explain human generosity in one-shot encounters. *Proceedings of the National Academy of Sciences, 108*(32), 13335–13340.

Demos, K. E., Kelley, W. M., & Heatherton, T. F. (2011). Dietary restraint violations influence reward responses in nucleus accumbens and amygdala. *Journal of Cognitive Neuroscience, 23*(8), 1952–1963.

Den Hartog, D. N., De Hoogh, A. H., & Belschak, F. D. (2018). Toot Your Own Horn? Leader narcissism and the effectiveness of employee self-promotion. *Journal of Management, 46*(2), 261–286.

Depue, R. A., & Collins, P. F. (1999). Neurobiology of the structure of personality: Dopamine, facilitation of incentive motivation, and extraversion. *Behavioral and Brain Sciences, 22*(3), 491–517.

DeYoung, C. G., Hirsh, J. B., Shane, M. S., Papademitris, X., Rajeevan, J., & Gray, J. R. (2010). Testing predictions from personality neuroscience: Brain structure and the Big Five. *Psychological Science, 21*(6), 820–828.

Dubois, J., Eberhardt, F., Paul, L. K., & Adolphs, R. (2020). Personality beyond taxonomy. *Nature Human Behaviour, 4*(11), 1110–1117.

Dunn, B. D., Galton, H. C., Morgan, R., Evans, D., Oliver, C., Meyer, M., . . . Dalgleish, T. (2010). Listening to your heart: How interoception shapes emotion experience and intuitive decision making. *Psychological Science, 21*(12), 1835–1844.

Eisenhower, D. D. (1954). *Remarks at the Annual Conference of the Society for Personnel Administration.* Dwight D. Eisenhower Presidential Library, Museum & Boyhood Home. https://www.eisenhowerlibrary.gov/media/3842

Ekman, P. (1993). Facial expression and emotion. *American Psychologist, 48,* 384–392.

Ekman, P., & Friesen, W. V. (1971). Constants across cultures in the face and emotion. *Journal of Personality and Social Psychology, 17*(2), 124–129.

Erickson, K. I., Voss, M. W., Prakash, R. S., Basak, C., Szabo, A., Chaddock, L., . . . Kramer, A. F. (2011). Exercise training increases size of hippocampus and improves memory. *Proceedings of the National Academy of Sciences, 108*(7), 3017–3022.

Evans, J. S. B. (2008). Dual-processing accounts of reasoning, judgment, and social cognition. *Annual Review of Psychology, 59,* 255–278.

Fehr, E., & Camerer, C. F. (2007). Social neuroeconomics: The neural circuitry of social preferences. *Trends in Cognitive Sciences, 11*(10), 419–427.

Fehr, E., & Gächter, S. (2002). Altruistic punishment in humans. *Nature, 415*(6868), 137–140.

Finucane, M. L., Alhakami, A., Slovic, P., & Johnson, S. M. (2000). The affect heuristic in judgments of risks and benefits. *Journal of Behavioral Decision Making, 13*, 1–17.

Fischbacher, U., Gächter, S., & Fehr, E. (2001). Are people conditionally cooperative? Evidence from a public goods experiment. *Economics Letters, 71*(3), 397–404.

Förster, J., & Higgins, E. T. (2005). How global versus local perception fits regulatory focus. *Psychological Science, 16*(8), 631–636.

Fredrickson, B. L., & Branigan, C. (2005). Positive emotions broaden the scope of attention and thought-action repertoires. *Cognition & Emotion, 19*(3), 313–332.

Gailliot, M. T., Baumeister, R. F., DeWall, C. N., Maner, J. K., Plant, E. A., Tice, D. M., ... Schmeichel, B. J. (2007). Self-control relies on glucose as a limited energy source: Willpower is more than a metaphor. *Journal of Personality and Social Psychology, 92*(2), 325–336.

Galinsky, A. D., Gruenfeld, D. H., & Magee, J. C. (2003). From power to action. *Journal of Personality and Social Psychology, 85*(3), 453–466.

Galinsky, A. D., Magee, J. C., Gruenfeld, D. H., Whitson, J. A., & Liljenquist, K. A. (2008). Power reduces the press of the situation: Implications for creativity, conformity, and dissonance. *Journal of Personality and Social Psychology, 95*(6), 1450–1466.

Galinsky, A. D., Magee, J. C., Inesi, M. E., & Gruenfeld, D. H. (2006). Power and perspectives not taken. *Psychological Science, 17*, 1068–1074.

Galvin, B., Waldman, D. A., & Balthazard, P. (2010). Visionary communication qualities as mediators of the relationship between narcissism and attributions of leader charisma. *Personnel Psychology, 63*, 509–537.

Gandhi, N. J., & Katnani, H. A. (2011). Motor functions of the superior colliculus. *Annual Review of Neuroscience, 34*, 205–231.

Gazzaniga, M. (2011). *Who's in charge? Free will and the science of the brain.* HarperCollins.

Gazzaniga, M. S., Ivry, R. B., & Mangun, G. R. (2014). *Cognitive neuroscience: The biology of the mind* (4th ed.). Norton & Company.

Gelfand, M. (2019). *Rule makers, rule breakers: Tight and loose cultures and the secret signals that direct our lives.* Simon and Schuster.

Gerlach, M., Farb, B., Revelle, W., & Nunes Amaral, L. A. (2018). A robust data-driven approach identifies four personality types across four large data sets. *Nature Human Behaviour, 2,* 735–742.

Gervais, S. J., Guinote, A., Allen, J., & Slabu, L. (2013). Power increases situated creativity. *Social Influence, 8*(4), 294–311.

Gigerenzer, G. (2007). *Gut feelings: The intelligence of the unconscious.* Penguin.

Giurge, L. M., van Dijke, M., Zheng, M. X., & De Cremer, D. (2021, August). Does power corrupt the mind? The influence of power on moral reasoning and self-interested behavior. *The Leadership Quarterly, 32*(4), 101288.

Golby, A. J., Gabrieli, J. D., Chiao, J. Y., & Eberhardt, J. L. (2001). Differential responses in the fusiform region to same-race and other-race faces. *Nature Neuroscience, 4*(8), 845–850.

Grant, V. J., & France, J. T. (2001). Dominance and testosterone in women. *Biological Psychology, 58*(1), 41–47.

Greene, J. D., Nystrom, L. E., Engell, A. D., Darley, J. M., & Cohen, J. D. (2004). The neural bases of cognitive conflict and control in moral judgment. *Neuron, 44*(2), 389–400.

Guastello, S. J., & Peressini, A. F. (2017). Development of a synchronization coefficient for biosocial interactions in groups and teams. *Small Group Research, 48*(1), 3–33.

Guinote, A. (2007). Power and goal pursuit. *Personality and Social Psychology Bulletin, 33*(8), 1076–1087.

Gu, X., Wang, X., Hula, A., Wang, S., Xu, S., Lohrenz, T. M., Knight, R. T., Gao, Z., Dayan, P., & Montague, P. R. (2015). Necessary, yet dissociable contributions of the insular and ventromedial prefrontal cortices to norm adaptation: Computational and lesion evidence in humans. *The Journal of Neuroscience, 35*(2), 467–473. https://doi.org/10.1523/jneurosci.2906-14.2015

Gu€rerk, O., Irlenbusch, B., & Rockenbach, B. (2006). The competitive advantage of sanctioning institutions. *Science, 312*(5770), 108–111.

Haidt, J. (2001). The emotional dog and its rational tail: A social intuitionist approach to moral judgment. *Psychological Review*, *108*(4), 814–834.

Hall, C. C., Ariss, L., & Todorov, A. (2007). The illusion of knowledge: When more information reduces accuracy and increases confidence. *Organizational Behavior and Human Decision Processes*, *103*(2), 277–290.

Ham, C., Seybert, N., & Wang, S. (2018). Narcissism is a bad sign: CEO signature size, investment, and performance. *Review of Accounting Studies*, *23*(1), 234–264.

Hamstra, M. R., Van Yperen, N. W., Wisse, B., & Sassenberg, K. (2011). Transformational-transactional leadership styles and followers' regulatory focus. *Journal of Personnel Psychology*, *10*, 187–191.

Harada, T., Bridge, D., & Chiao, J. Y. (2013). Dynamic social power modulates neural basis of math calculation. *Frontiers in Human Neuroscience*, *6*(350), 115–127.

Hartl, A. C., Laursen, B., Cantin, S., & Vitaro, F. (2020). A test of the bistrategic control hypothesis of adolescent popularity. *Child Development*, *9*(3), e635–e648.

Haselhuhn, M. P., & Wong, E. M. (2011). Bad to the bone: Facial structure predicts unethical behaviour. *Proceedings of the Royal Society B: Biological Sciences*, *279*(1728), 571–576.

Heilbron, M., Armeni, K., Schoffelen, J. M., Hagoort, P., & De Lange, F. P. (2022). A hierarchy of linguistic predictions during natural language comprehension. *Proceedings of the National Academy of Sciences*, *119*(32), e2201968119.

Heyden, M. L., Gu, J., Wechtler, H. M., & Ekanayake, U. I. (2022). The face of wrongdoing? An expectancy violations perspective on CEO facial characteristics and media coverage of misconducting firms. *The Leadership Quarterly*, 101671.

Hietanen, J. K., Myllyneva, A., Helminen, T. M., & Lyyra, P. (2018). Affective eye contact: An integrative review. *Frontiers in Psychology*, *9*, 1587.

Hirsch, J., Zhang, X., Noah, J. A., & Ono, Y. (2017). Frontal temporal and parietal systems synchronize within and across brains during live eye-to-eye contact. *NeuroImage*, *157*, 314–330.

Hogeveen, J., Inzlicht, M., & Obhi, S. S. (2014). Power changes how the brain responds to others. *Journal of Experimental Psychology: General, 143*(2), 755–762.

Jessen, S., & Grossmann, T. (2016). Neural and behavioral evidence for infants' sensitivity to the trustworthiness of faces. *Journal of Cognitive Neuroscience, 28*(11), 1728–1736.

Jiang, J., Chen, C., Dai, B., Shi, G., Ding, G., Liu, L., & Lu, C. (2015). Leader emergence through interpersonal neural synchronization. *Proceedings of the National Academy of Sciences, 112*(14), 4274–4279.

Johnson, M. D., Awtrey, E., & Ong, W. J. (2022). Verdicts, elections, and counterterrorism: When groups take unofficial votes. *Academy of Management Discoveries.* https://doi.org/10.5465/amd.2021.0099

Johnston, E., & Olson, L. (2015). *The feeling brain: The biology and psychology of emotions.* W. W. Norton & Company.

Judge, T. A., Bono, J. E., Ilies, R., & Gerhardt, M. W. (2002). Personality and leadership: A qualitative and quantitative review. *Journal of Applied Psychology, 87*(4), 765–780.

Just, M. A., & Carpenter, P. A. (1992). A capacity theory of comprehension: Individual differences in working memory. *Psychological Review, 99*(1), 122–149.

Kahneman, D., & Klein, G. (2009). Conditions for intuitive expertise: A failure to disagree. *American Psychologist, 64*(6), 515–526.

Kamiya, S., Kawakita, G., Sasai, S., Kitazono, J., & Oizumi, M. (2023). Optimal control costs of brain state transitions in linear stochastic systems. *Journal of Neuroscience, 43*(2), 270–281.

Kanwisher, N., & Yovel, G. (2006). The fusiform face area: A cortical region specialized for the perception of faces. *Philosophical Transactions of the Royal Society B: Biological Sciences, 361*(1476), 2109–2128.

Kao, A. B., & Couzin, I. D. (2014). Decision accuracy in complex environments is often maximized by small group sizes. *Proceedings of the Royal Society B: Biological Sciences, 281*(1784), 20133305.

Kassin, S. M., & Kiechel, K. L. (1996). The social psychology of false confessions: Compliance, internalization, and confabulation. *Psychological Science, 7*(3), 125–128.

Kawasaki, M., Yamada, Y., Ushiku, Y., Miyauchi, E., & Yamaguchi, Y. (2013). Inter-brain synchronization during coordination of speech rhythm in human-to-human social interaction. *Scientific Reports*, *3*(1), 1692.

Keltner, D. (2017). *The power paradox: How we gain and lose influence.* Penguin Books.

Keltner, D., & Haidt, J. (1999). Social functions of emotions at four levels of analysis. *Cognition & Emotion*, *13*(5), 505–521.

Keltner, D., & Haidt, J. (2003). Approaching awe, a moral, spiritual, and aesthetic emotion. *Cognition & Emotion*, *17*(2), 297–314.

Keltner, D., Oatley, K., & Jenkins, J. M. (2014). *Understanding emotions.* Wiley.

Kim, Y., & Na, J. (2020). The Olympic paradox: The Olympics and intergroup biases. *Group Processes & Intergroup Relations*, *25*(1), 26–43. https://doi.org/10.1177/1368430220931160

Kini, P., Wang, Y. J., McInnis, S., & Brown, J. (2016). The effects of gratitude expression on neural activity. *NeuroImage*, *128*, 1–10.

Kosfeld, M., Heinrichs, M., Zak, P. J., Fischbacher, U., & Fehr, E. (2005). Oxytocin increases trust in humans. *Nature*, *435*, 673–625.

Krueger, F., McCabe, K., Moll, J., Kriegeskorte, N., Zahn, R., Strenziok, M., … Grafman, J. (2007). Neural correlates of trust. *Proceedings of the National Academy of Sciences*, *104*(50), 20084–20089.

Kruglanski, A. W., Bélanger, J. J., Chen, X., Köpetz, C., Pierro, A., & Mannetti, L. (2012). The energetics of motivated cognition: A force-field analysis. *Psychological Review*, *119*(1), 1–20.

Kuo, W. J., Sjöström, T., Chen, Y. P., Wang, Y. H., & Huang, C. Y. (2009). Intuition and deliberation: Two systems for strategizing in the brain. *Science*, *324*(5926), 519–522.

Kuzawa, C. W., Chugani, H. T., Grossman, L. I., Lipovich, L., Muzik, O., Hof, P. R., … Lange, N. (2014). Metabolic costs and evolutionary implications of human brain development. *Proceedings of the National Academy of Sciences*, *111*(36), 13010–13015.

Lammers, J., Stoker, J. I., Rink, F., & Galinsky, A. D. (2016). To have control over or to be free from others? The desire for power reflects a need for autonomy. *Personality and Social Psychology Bulletin*, *42*(4), 498–512.

Latham, G. P., & Locke, E. A. (1991). Self regulation through goal setting. *Organizational Behavior and Human Decision Processes, 50*(2), 212–247.

Lau, H. C., Rogers, R. D., & Passingham, R. E. (2007). Manipulating the experienced onset of intention after action execution. *Journal of Cognitive Neuroscience, 19*(1), 81–90.

Lefevre, C. E., Lewis, G. J., Perrett, D. I., & Penke, L. (2013). Telling facial metrics: Facial width is associated with testosterone levels in men. *Evolution and Human Behavior, 34*(4), 273–279.

Lerner, J. S., Li, Y., Valdesolo, P., & Kassam, K. S. (2015). Emotion and decision making. *Annual Review of Psychology, 66*, 799–823.

Levy, D. J., & Glimcher, P. W. (2012). The root of all value: A neural common currency for choice. *Current Opinion in Neurobiology, 22*(6), 1027–1038.

Li, W., Arvey, R. D., Zhang, Z., & Song, Z. (2012). Do leadership role occupancy and transformational leadership share the same genetic and environmental influences? *The Leadership Quarterly, 23*(2), 233–243.

Lieberman, M. D. (2000). Intuition: A social cognitive neuroscience approach. *Psychological Bulletin, 126*(1), 109–137.

Li, J., Tian, M., Fang, H., Xu, M., Li, H., & Liu, J. (2010). Extraversion predicts individual differences in face recognition. *Communicative & Integrative Biology, 3*(4), 295–298.

Li, W. D., Wang, N., Arvey, R. D., Soong, R., Saw, S. M., & Song, Z. (2015). A mixed blessing? Dual mediating mechanisms in the relationship between dopamine transporter gene DAT1 and leadership role occupancy. *The Leadership Quarterly, 26*(5), 671–686.

Loehlin, J. C., McCrae, R. R., Costa, P. T., Jr., & John, O. P. (1998). Heritabilities of common and measure-specific components of the Big Five personality factors. *Journal of Research in Personality, 32*(4), 431–453.

Loftus, E. F. (1991). Made in memory: Distortions in recollection after misleading information. *Psychology of Learning and Motivation, 27*, 187–215.

Magistretti, P. J., & Allaman, I. (2015). A cellular perspective on brain energy metabolism and functional imaging. *Neuron, 86*(4), 883–901.

Mathur, V. A., Harada, T., Lipke, T., & Chiao, J. Y. (2010). Neural basis of extraordinary empathy and altruistic motivation. *NeuroImage, 51*(4), 1468–1475.

McMullen, J. S., Shepherd, D. A., & Patzelt, H. (2009). Managerial (in) attention to competitive threats. *Journal of Management Studies, 46*(2), 157–181.

Miller, C. E. (1985). Group decision making under majority and unanimity decision rules. *Social Psychology Quarterly, 48*(1), 51–61.

Miller, C. C., & Ireland, R. D. (2005). Intuition in strategic decision making: Friend or foe in the fast-paced 21st century? *Academy of Management Perspectives, 19*(1), 19–30.

Mitchell, R. L., Bae, K. K., Case, C. R., & Hays, N. A. (2020). Drivers of desire for social rank. *Current Opinion in Psychology, 33*, 189–195.

Morgan, D., Grant, K. A., Gage, H. D., Mach, R. H., Kaplan, J. R., Prioleau, O., ... Nader, M. A. (2002). Social dominance in monkeys: Dopamine D 2 receptors and cocaine self-administration. *Nature Neuroscience, 5*(2), 169–174.

Navajas, J., Niella, T., Garbulsky, G., Bahrami, B., & Sigman, M. (2018). Aggregated knowledge from a small number of debates outperforms the wisdom of large crowds. *Nature Human Behaviour, 2*(2), 126–132.

Nissan, T., Shapira, O., & Liberman, N. (2015). Effects of power on mental rotation and emotion recognition in women. *Personality and Social Psychology Bulletin, 41*(10), 1425–1437.

Oakes, L. M. (2017). Plasticity may change inputs as well as processes, structures, and responses. *Cognitive Development, 42*, 4–14.

Öhman, A. (2005). The role of the amygdala in human fear: Automatic detection of threat. *Psychoneuroendocrinology, 30*(10), 953–958.

Oh, D., Shafir, E., & Todorov, A. (2019). Economic status cues from clothes affect perceived competence from faces. *Nature Human Behaviour,* 1–7.

Özugur, S., Kunz, L., & Straka, H. (2020). Relationship between oxygen consumption and neuronal activity in a defined neural circuit. *BMC Biology, 18*(1), 1–16.

Palmer, C. J., & Clifford, C. W. (2020). Face pareidolia recruits mechanisms for detecting human social attention. *Psychological Science, 31*(8), 1001–1012.

Panchanathan, K., & Boyd, R. (2004). Indirect reciprocity can stabilize cooperation without the second-order free rider problem. *Nature, 432*(7016), 499–502.

Parameshwaran, D., Sathishkumar, S., & Thiagarajan, T. C. (2021). The impact of socioeconomic and stimulus inequality on human brain physiology. *Scientific Reports, 11*(1). https://doi.org/10.1038/s41598-021-85236-z

Parkinson, C., Kleinbaum, A. M., & Wheatley, T. (2017). Spontaneous neural encoding of social network position. *Nature Human Behaviour, 1*(5), 1–7.

Park, T. Y., Park, S., & Barry, B. (2022). Incentive effects on ethics. *The Academy of Management Annals, 16*(1), 297–333.

Paulhus, D. L., & Williams, K. M. (2002). The Dark Triad of personality: Narcissism, Machiavellianism, and psychopathy. *Journal of Research in Personality, 36, 556–563.*

Piazza, E. A., Hasenfratz, L., Hasson, U., & Lew-Williams, C. (2020). Infant and adult brains are coupled to the dynamics of natural communication. *Psychological Science, 31*(1), 6–17.

Piff, P. K., Stancato, D. M., Côté, S., Mendoza-Denton, R., & Keltner, D. (2012). Higher social class predicts increased unethical behavior. *Proceedings of the National Academy of Sciences, 109*(11), 4086–4091.

Pratto, F. (2015). On power and empowerment. *British Journal of Social Psychology, 55*(1), 1–20. https://doi.org/10.1111/bjso.12135

Pratto, F., & John, O. P. (1991). Automatic vigilance: The attention-grabbing power of negative social information. *Journal of Personality and Social Psychology, 61*(3), 380–391.

Prundeanu, O., Constantin, T., & Popuşoi, S. A. (2021). Climb up your ego! Narcissistic status pursuit and motivation to lead. *Personality and Individual Differences, 177,* 110830.

Raichle, M. E., & Gusnard, D. A. (2002). Appraising the brain's energy budget. *Proceedings of the National Academy of Sciences, 99*(16), 10237–10239.

Rand, D. G., Greene, J. D., & Nowak, M. A. (2012). Spontaneous giving and calculated greed. *Nature, 489*(7416), 427–430.

Rand, D. G., Newman, G. E., & Wurzbacher, O. M. (2015). Social context and the dynamics of cooperative choice. *Journal of Behavioral Decision Making, 28*(2), 159–166.

Rand, D. G., & Nowak, M. A. (2013). Human cooperation. *Trends in Cognitive Sciences, 17*(8), 413–425.

Rand, D. G., Peysakhovich, A., Kraft-Todd, G. T., Newman, G. E., Wurzbacher, O., Nowak, M. A., & Greene, J. D. (2014). Social heuristics shape intuitive cooperation. *Nature Communications*, *5*(1). Article Number 3677.

Reichard, R. J., Riggio, R. E., Guerin, D. W., Oliver, P. H., Gottfried, A. W., & Gottfried, A. E. (2011). A longitudinal analysis of relationships between adolescent personality and intelligence with adult leader emergence and transformational leadership. *The Leadership Quarterly*, *22*(3), 471–481.

Reimann, M., Schilke, O., & Cook, K. S. (2017). Trust is heritable, whereas distrust is not. *Proceedings of the National Academy of Sciences*, *114*(27), 7007–7012.

Rizzolatti, G., & Sinigaglia, C. (2010). The functional role of the parieto-frontal mirror circuit: Interpretations and misinterpretations. *Nature Reviews Neuroscience*, *11*(4), 264–274.

Rubinstein, J. S., Meyer, D. E., & Evans, J. E. (2001). Executive control of cognitive processes in task switching. *Journal of Experimental Psychology: Human Perception and Performance*, *27*(4), 763–797.

Rule, N. O., Adams, R. B., Jr., Ambady, N., & Freeman, J. B. (2012). Perceptions of dominance following glimpses of faces and bodies. *Perception*, *41*(6), 687–706.

Rule, N. O., & Ambady, N. (2008). The face of success: Inferences from chief executive officers' appearance predict company profits. *Psychological Science*, *19*, 109–111.

Ryding, S., Garnham, L. C., Abbey-Lee, R. N., Petkova, I., Kreshchenko, A., & Løvlie, H. (2021). Impulsivity is affected by cognitive enrichment and links to brain gene expression in red junglefowl chicks. *Animal Behaviour*, *178*, 195–207.

Salimpoor, V. N., van den Bosch, I., Kovacevic, N., McIntosh, A. R., Dagher, A., & Zatorre, R. J. (2013). Interactions between the nucleus accumbens and auditory cortices predict music reward value. *Science*, *340*(6129), 216–219.

Sanfey, A. G., Rilling, J. K., Aronson, J. A., Nystrom, L. E., & Cohen, J. D. (2003). The neural basis of economic decision-making in the Ultimatum Game. *Science*, *300*(5626), 1755–1758.

Sangrigoli, S., & De Schonen, S. (2004). Recognition of own-race and other-race faces by three-month-old infants. *Journal of Child Psychology and Psychiatry*, *45*(7), 1219–1227.

Schacter, D. L. (2002). *The seven sins of memory: How the mind forgets and remembers*. HMH.

Scheepers, D., de Wit, F., Ellemers, N., & Sassenberg, K. (2012). Social power makes the heart work more efficiently: Evidence from cardiovascular markers of challenge and threat. *Journal of Experimental Social Psychology, 48*(1), 371–374.

Schmid, P. C., & Amodio, D. M. (2017). Power effects on implicit prejudice and stereotyping: The role of intergroup face processing. *Social Neuroscience, 12*(2), 218–231.

Schultheiss, O. C., & Schiepe-Tiska, A. (2013). The role of the dorsoanterior striatum in implicit motivation: The case of the need for power. *Frontiers in Human Neuroscience, 7*, 141.

Schultheiss, O. C., Wirth, M. M., Torges, C. M., Pang, J. S., Villacorta, M. A., & Welsh, K. M. (2005). Effects of implicit power motivation on men's and women's implicit learning and testosterone changes after social victory or defeat. *Journal of Personality and Social Psychology, 88*(1), 174–188.

Schultz, W. (2016). Dopamine reward prediction-error signalling: A two-component response. *Nature Reviews Neuroscience, 17*(3), 183–195.

Shadlen, M. N., & Shohamy, D. (2016). Decision making and sequential sampling from memory. *Neuron, 90*(5), 927–939.

Shanteau, J. (1992). Competence in experts: The role of task characteristics. *Organizational Behavior and Human Decision Processes, 53*, 252–262.

Siemer, M., Mauss, I., & Gross, J. J. (2007). Same situation–different emotions: How appraisals shape our emotions. *Emotion, 7*(3), 592–600.

Silfwerbrand, L., Ogata, Y., Yoshimura, N., Koike, Y., & Gingnell, M. (2023). An fMRI-study of leading and following using rhythmic tapping. *Social Neuroscience*. https://doi.org/10.1080/17470919.2023.2189615

Singer, T., Seymour, B., O'Doherty, J., Kaube, H., Dolan, R. J., & Frith, C. D. (2004). Empathy for pain involves the affective but not sensory components of pain. *Science, 303*(5661), 1157–1162.

Smith, S. M., & Krajbich, I. (2018). Attention and choice across domains. *Journal of Experimental Psychology: General, 147*(12), 1810–1826.

Smith, P. K., & Trope, Y. (2006). You focus on the forest when you're in charge of the trees: Power priming and abstract information processing. *Journal of Personality and Social Psychology, 90*(4), 578–596.

Spangler, W. D., Tikhomirov, A., Sotak, K. L., & Palrecha, R. (2014). Leader motive profiles in eight types of organizations. *The Leadership Quarterly*, *25*(6), 1080–1094.

Stanek, K. C., & Ones, D. S. (2023). Meta-analytic relations between personality and cognitive ability. *Proceedings of the National Academy of Sciences*, *120*(23), e2212794120.

Staudigl, T., Minxha, J., Mamelak, A. N., Gothard, K. M., & Rutishauser, U. (2022). Saccade-related neural communication in the human medial temporal lobe is modulated by the social relevance of stimuli. *Science Advances*, *8*(11), eabl6037.

Strang, S. E., & Kuhnert, K. W. (2009). Personality and leadership developmental levels as predictors of leader performance. *The Leadership Quarterly*, *20*(3), 421–433.

Sturm, R. E., & Antonakis, J. (2015). Interpersonal power: A review, critique, and research agenda. *Journal of Management*, *41*(1), 136–163.

Sutton, S. K., & Davidson, R. J. (2000). Prefrontal brain electrical asymmetry predicts the evaluation of affective stimuli. *Neuropsychologia*, *38*, 1723–1733.

Tabatabaeian, M., Dale, R., & Duran, N. D. (2015). Self-serving dishonest decisions can show facilitated cognitive dynamics. *Cognitive Processing*, *16*, 291–300.

Tabibnia, G., Satpute, A. B., & Lieberman, M. D. (2008). The sunny side of fairness preference for fairness activates reward circuitry (and disregarding unfairness activates self-control circuitry). *Psychological Science*, *19*(4), 339–347.

Telzer, E. H., Flannery, J., Shapiro, M., Humphreys, K. L., Goff, B., Gabard-Durman, L., ... Tottenham, N. (2013). Early experience shapes amygdala sensitivity to race: An international adoption design. *Journal of Neuroscience*, *33*(33), 13484–13488.

Thagard, P. (2012). *The brain and the meaning of life*. Princeton University Press.

Thomas, R. M., Hotsenpiller, G., & Peterson, D. A. (2007). Acute psychosocial stress reduces cell survival in adult hippocampal neurogenesis without altering proliferation. *Journal of Neuroscience*, *27*(11), 2734–2743.

Thomas, K. W., & Velthouse, B. A. (1990). Cognitive elements of empowerment: An "interpretive" model of intrinsic task motivation. *Academy of Management Review, 15*(4), 666–681.

Todorov, A., Mandisodza, A. N., Goren, A., & Hall, C. C. (2005). Inferences of competence from faces predict election outcomes. *Science, 308*(5728), 1623–1626.

Todorov, A., Pakrashi, M., & Oosterhof, N. N. (2009). Evaluating faces on trustworthiness after minimal time exposure. *Social Cognition, 27*(6), 813–833.

Tost, L. P., Gino, F., & Larrick, R. P. (2012). Power, competitiveness, and advice taking: Why the powerful don't listen. *Organizational Behavior and Human Decision Processes, 117*(1), 53–65.

Turkheimer, E. (2000). Three laws of behavior genetics and what they mean. *Current Directions in Psychological Science, 9*(5), 160–164.

Van Bavel, J. J., & Packer, D. J. (2021). *The power of us: Harnessing our shared identities to improve performance, increase cooperation, and promote social harmony.* Little.

Van Bavel, J. J., Pärnamets, P., Reinero, D. A., & Packer, D. (2022). How neurons, norms, and institutions shape group cooperation. *Advances in Experimental Social Psychology, 66*, 59–105.

Van Berkum, J. J., Holleman, B., Nieuwland, M., Otten, M., & Murre, J. (2009). Right or wrong? The brain's fast response to morally objectionable statements. *Psychological Science, 20*(9), 1092–1099.

Van Cappellen, P., Ladd, K. L., Cassidy, S., Edwards, M. E., & Fredrickson, B. L. (2022). Bodily feedback: Expansive and upward posture facilitates the experience of positive affect. *Cognition & Emotion, 36*(7), 1327–1342.

Van Kleef, G. A., Oveis, C., Homan, A. C., van der Löwe, I., & Keltner, D. (2015). Power gets you high: The powerful are more inspired by themselves than by others. *Social Psychological and Personality Science, 6*(4), 472–480.

Van der Meij, L., Schaveling, J., & van Vugt, M. (2016). Basal testosterone, leadership and dominance: A field study and meta-analysis. *Psychoneuroendocrinology, 72*, 72–79.

Veroude, K., Norris, D. G., Shumskaya, E., Gullberg, M., & Indefrey, P. (2010). Functional connectivity between brain regions involved in learning words of a new language. *Brain and Language, 113*(1), 21–27.

Vitanova, I. (2021). Nurturing overconfidence: The relationship between leader power, overconfidence and firm performance. *The Leadership Quarterly, 32*(4), 101342.

Voelcker-Rehage, C., & Niemann, C. (2013). Structural and functional brain changes related to different types of physical activity across the life span. *Neuroscience & Biobehavioral Reviews, 37*(9), 2268–2295.

Wagner, A. D., Poldrack, R. A., Eldridge, L., Desmond, J. E., Glover, G. H., & Gabrieli, J. D. E. (1998). Material-specific lateralization of prefrontal activation during episodic encoding and retrieval. *NeuroReport, 9,* 3711–3713.

Wallach, W., & Allen, C. (2009). *Moral machines: Teaching robots right from wrong.* https://doi.org/10.1604/9780195374049

Wang, Y. (2019). Pulling at your heartstrings: Examining four leadership approaches from the neuroscience perspective. *Educational Administration Quarterly, 55*(2), 328–359.

Wang, Y. (2021). What is the role of emotions in educational leaders' decision making? Proposing an organizing framework. *Educational Administration Quarterly, 57*(3), 372–402.

Wang, L., Restubog, S., Shao, B., Lu, V., & Van Kleef, G. A. (2018). Does anger expression help or harm leader effectiveness? The role of competence-based versus integrity-based violations and abusive supervision. *Academy of Management Journal, 61*(3), 1050–1072.

Watson, D., & Clark, L. A. (1984). Negative affectivity: The disposition to experience negative emotional states. *Psychological Bulletin, 96,* 465–490.

Weick, M., & Guinote, A. (2008). When subjective experiences matter: Power increases reliance on the ease of retrieval. *Journal of Personality and Social Psychology, 94*(6), 956–970.

White, R. E., Thornhill, S., & Hampson, E. (2006). Entrepreneurs and evolutionary biology: The relationship between testosterone and new venture creation. *Organizational Behavior and Human Decision Processes, 100*(1), 21–34.

Whitson, J. A., Liljenquist, K. A., Galinsky, A. D., Magee, J. C., Gruenfeld, D. H., & Cadena, B. (2013). The blind leading: Power reduces awareness of constraints. *Journal of Experimental Social Psychology, 49*(3), 579–582.

Wilkins, A. S. (2017). *Making faces.* Harvard University Press.

Williams, P. (2020). Wells Fargo to pay $3 billion over fake account scandal. *NBC News.* https://www.nbcnews.com/news/all/wells-fargo-pay-3-billion-over-fake-account-scandal-n1140541

Willis, G. B., Rodríguez-Bailón, R., & Lupiáñez, J. (2011). The boss is paying attention: Power affects the functioning of the attentional networks. *Social Cognition, 29*(2), 166–181.

Wilson, D. S., Near, D., & Miller, R. R. (1998). Individual differences in Machiavellianism as a mix of cooperative and exploitive strategies. *Evolution and Human Behavior, 19*, 203–212.

Winter, D. G. (1973). *The power motive.* Free Press.

Wong, E. M., Ormiston, M. E., & Haselhuhn, M. P. (2011). A face only an investor could love: CEOs' facial structure predicts their firms' financial performance. *Psychological Science, 22*(12), 1478–1483.

Xu, M., Morimoto, S., Hoshino, E., Suzuki, K., & Minagawa, Y. (2023). Two-in-one system and behavior-specific brain synchrony during goal-free cooperative creation: An analytical approach combining automated behavioral classification and the event-related generalized linear model. *Neurophotonics, 10*(1), 013511.

Yukl, G. A., & Becker, W. S. (2006). Effective empowerment in organizations. *Organization Management Journal, 3*(3), 210–231.

Zhong, C. B. (2011). The ethical dangers of deliberative decision making. *Administrative Science Quarterly, 56*(1), 1–25.

Zucker, L. G. (1986). Production of trust: Institutional sources of economic structure, 1840–1920. *Research in Organizational Behavior, 8*, 53–111.

Printed in the USA
CPSIA information can be obtained
at www.ICGtesting.com
JSHW052030080224
56946JS00004B/31